At a Stroke
Diary of a Recovery

by

Stephen Trombley

At a Stroke: Diary of a Recovery

First published in France in 2018 by Worldview Pictures

Copyright © Stephen Trombley 2018

The moral right of Stephen Trombley to be identified as the author of this work has been asserted by him in accordance with the Copyright, Designs and Patents Act, 1998.

All rights reserved. No part of this book may be reproduced by any means, electronic or mechanical, including photocopy or any information storage and retrieval system without permission in writing from the copyright owner and publisher of this book.

Design: Debi Warford Design

Photography: Charlie Kaser

Chez Louainet
16480 Brossac
France
stephen.trombley@gmail.com

For WT Davidson, whose friendship is unconditional.

At a Stroke: Diary of a Recovery

The worst thing about being paralyzed is having to ask someone else to wipe your ass.

Acknowledgments

No one expects a stroke.

It's one of those things that happen to other people. Until the moment when you are not like 'other people' but become one of us – a person who *is* a stroke.

It is a profound lesson in humility.

Andrew Holt, my oldest UK friend, came from Jersey to visit me as soon as he heard. My brother, Brian, came from New Hampshire. He took charge of the house in my absence and welcomed Kay Francis, who looked after me with kindness and affection for several months upon my release from hospital.

My agent, Toby Mundy, has been an unwavering source of encouragement and I think he would probably be a little embarrassed if he knew how much I have valued it.

My friends on Facebook have been faithful readers of sections of this text in draft form and many of them helped support my work by purchasing copies of the draft typescript. I would not have survived the winter of 2018 if not for them.

I will always be grateful to the nurses and nursing assistants who cared for me.

This is a memoir. All of the events depicted here are true. Some names and identifying details have been changed.

This book probably contains typographical errors.

Stephen Trombley
Brossac
France

CONTENTS

Accident

Patients

Reeducation

Expulsion

Progress

Recovery

At a Stroke: Diary of a Recovery

Accident

Casualty in a French hospital is marked by an absence of noise and unnecessary drama.

US medics must, I think, take comfort in the volume of sound they generate as if it somehow relates to useful effort. Your French medical staff by contrast seem more concentrated on the task in hand: setting an IV, measuring blood pressure, taking an ECG, performing a brain scan. Because the French team is quiet and unpanicky I can listen to what they say and learn the French words that describe my condition.

For instance, learn that I have suffered an AVC (*accident vasculaire cérébral* – a stroke when it's at home). I learn this as a nurse with a man bun expertly (ie, painlessly and on his first try) inserts an intravenous drip (*perfusion*) in my left arm. His colleague takes my blood pressure (*tension*) and makes a face which conveys the universal meaning 'Are you kidding me? This fucker's not still alive, is he?'

*

Nashville was nice but it was not heaven right here on Earth.

Everyone knows heaven is in France.

My partner's inability to speak the language and lack of the right to live here were minor obstacles that were overcome by some YouTube language lessons and a visa. (I am a citizen of the UK – and therefore, Europe. I retain my original US nationality).

My partner and I had been considering expatriation for about a year. We entertained (for a very short time) the idea of moving to Guatemala. Guam. Grenada. But it was always going to be France; I was just waiting for my mate Martin to offer me his place in the Charente for a peppercorn rent in exchange for looking after it. (What were the chances, eh?)

My partner drove to Atlanta to apply for the visa. She then put on a garage sale while I travelled to France to establish a forward operating base at a truck stop outside of Fignac (an hour north of Bordeaux).

Martin and I and a very handy recording engineer friend from Nashville set about installing a kitchen and knocking the house into shape before occupying it. The lads stayed ten days after which I carried on painting and decorating. My son Ollie came for Christmas to help me get ready on the domestic front. My partner and my brother Brian arrived a few days later.

*

I can tell I've had another stroke soon after being admitted to hospital because my right arm is now paralyzed. Dead. No feeling. I look at it. It is an arm alright; it just didn't feel like mine. Actually, it doesn't even look like mine. But there it is, attached to the end of my shoulder.

I say another stroke because the neurologist has just been and mentioned that I have had several strokes. *Many strokes.* (How many, I don't know; nor does he, and what difference does it make, anyway?)

Dr Marc Gaillard is *chef de service* of the neurology department (from the get go I am aware of the quality of care I am receiving). He is tall for a Frenchman. In two weeks it will be Easter and Dr Gaillard will return from the break having had his hair cut. He will look very boyish and this is how I will remember him.

Dr Gaillard tells me that my case is 'very complicated'. It is marked, he says, by complications. Dr Gaillard does not speak the best English, but then I don't speak the best French.

*

Here is a fascinating (at least, to me) thing. Dr Gaillard and I have a limited vocabulary of words in common. But those words include ones like *cardiovasculaire* and *ataxie*. Our conversation is at once childlike and pedantic, stilted and eloquent. Our language is perfect for the task. I never feel as if I want to check his meaning. That our conversation concerns matters of life and death is understood and unquestioned. Yes, it is clear that I have suffered several heart attacks in addition to some strokes. Yes, I understand why the damage from the infarcts must be repaired first. I understand that at least three months must elapse between the heart operation (stents) and the stroke operation (carotid repair). I understand the risk of another catastrophic stroke during surgery.

I am already used to this arterial apocalypse.

*

Since being admitted to hospital I have been worried about Dr Gaillard's diagnosis/prognosis; but not as much as I have been worried about the fact that I have been conducting an affair and am terrified that my partner will discover it.

Will she look at my email?

Maybe has already, and is just biding her time.

*

My worry is obsessive.

And comprehensive.

I am in a panic. But I am paralyzed and can do nothing about it.

I am more confused than I've ever been. (My brains are scrambled).

I have I left my laptop at home, unsecured.

I am a keystroke away from 'fixing' the 'problem'. From 'cleaning up' my 'mess'.

From erasing the evidence of my treachery.

*

Dr Gaillard conducts his rounds in the traditional way, with a nurse standing behind him, just off his right shoulder. Her name is Renée and she is the prettiest nurse on the ward. (She is more than pretty, she is beautiful.)

When I wake, if I am lucky, Renée is the first thing I see in the morning. She wakes me by taking my blood. I dit bonjour. She beams at me and tugs my arm towards hers until my fingers are brushing her breast. She ignores it, pulls my hand a little closer. 'I prick you!', she bubbles. I close my eyes and wait for the pain. When she does it, it is delicious. Thick, red blood spurts from my arm into the vial.

And then she is done with me. She snaps the tourniquet off, clanks her bloodwork gear into the pan, flexes my arm into clotting position, fixes the bandage and leaves me bathed in the enduring glow of her smile.

When assisting Dr Gaillard she does not speak. She looks at him, not me. She is serious, nodding her understanding as she acknowledges his instructions. Then Dr Gaillard wishes me *bon courage* and is gone.

And then I remember all the things I wanted to ask him this morning.

Having a stroke means you can't remember shit (trying to remember only makes it worse). I could leave myself a note. If only I could remember how to read and write….

*

Hospital routine is unbending. Without strict routine – no exceptions to the rules – a hospital would descend into chaos. I like the routine. You know where you are with a hospital. You know what time breakfast will arrive: same time as yesterday, ie, in four hours.

Hospital night shift ends with an annoying and noisy *look at me I'm working* last visit from the staff. (They travel in pairs. On cold nights they are incognito, wearing patient gowns over their uniforms.) If they want to be particularly annoying they will choose this moment to take your temperature (in your ear, reminding you of Richard Pryor's encounter with a monkey if you are old enough to remember). Maybe they will take the opportunity noisily to rinse out your piss jug.

At a Stroke: Diary of a Recovery

*

Daybreak.

Clanking noises can mean a lot of different things in hospital: walking sticks, breakfast trolley, medical utensils dropped into those kidney-shaped bowls. Morning clanking after blood-taking generally signifies the arrival of the blood pressure trolley. Blood taking, blood pressure measurement and all that stuff exists only to raise excitement about breakfast; anticipation of it. I love taking breakfast in French hospitals. Not because it's the only meal of the day they can't fuck up (because they *can* fuck it up). Right now I wish I were in a French hospital stirring the clumpy, undissolved powdered milk in a plastic bowl of instant coffee.

Because then I would know what was supposed to happen next.

*

Nurse: 'What is the date?'

Long pause while I work out a landmark date: my brother's birthday. St Patrick's Day. Which was recent.

Me: 'March.'

Nurse: 'March the what?'

Real panic sets in. I think I might be going red in the face with the effort of remembering.

Nurse: 'It is April.'

Me: 'Oh.'

Fuck. Close though, right?

Nurse: 'April the what? What is the date?' She is shouting at me like I am deaf and an idiot. (I can hear perfectly well). I like nurses, but I don't like them shouting these kind of impossible questions. It is like when monolingual English people screech at the top of their lungs at monolingual foreigners. As if turning up the volume will aid comprehension.

I shrug my shoulders and make a stab at it. *St Patrick's Day has already been. That was on the seventeenth. Go on, take a guess. No. What is the point?*

Me: 'I have no idea.'

Nurse: 'It is the seventh of April.'

'Oh,' I say, as if it doesn't matter when it really, really does. Am I going to be one of those people about whom others remark derisively, *why ask him? He doesn't even know what time it is.* Yesterday people paid me, I had value, because of what I knew. Now I didn't know shit.

I wait a moment for panic to set in. But it doesn't. I give it another moment. No panic. Instead I find myself smiling at the realization I do not know what day it is or what the fuck is going on.

Nurse: 'The year?'

Me: 'I beg your pardon?'

Nurse: 'What year is it?'

Ridiculous question.

Me: 'It's... Hold on a minute.. It's...2015.'

Nurse: '2017.'

Oh.

*

It is time to bathe.

I can't think of anything cleverer than a bed bath. Just how do those nurses do it? Fit the sheet beneath you when you never leave the the bed? And so perfectly!

I think it is clever of the hospital, the way they schedule bed changing and other duties to do with *la toilette intime* (ie, personal hygiene relating to the *down there* department) so that no one nurse is burdened with the sights and smells of it for more than two days in a row.

I know that some readers will, at this juncture wonder about sexual arousal: the problem of unsolicited erections, hards-on, boners, stiffies, chubbies. I can report that I was untroubled by such, at least while receiving bed baths. (Later I was very relieved to experience my first post-stroke erection.) I was glad to remember the primary use of my right hand, but frustrated to remember that I am paralyzed. It will take a while to learn to wank with my left hand. (I am now ambidextrous.)

Having a paralyzed hand is something you can't avoid with strokes. It's not just wanking, but also eating that is compromised. Let's revisit the daily routine again, but remembering paralysis. (You'd be surprised what evasive actions you will take to avoid using your paralyzed right hand. And you will be mightily surprised the first time you have to wipe your ass.)

Firstly, you cannot eat without putting food all down the front of your hospital gown. (Did I mention that the 'bed rest' part of my treatment means no movement; ie, I am not allowed to move the unparalyzed parts of my body; I am not even allowed to sit in a wheelchair. Or what? *Or you'll have another stroke and this time you'll never walk again. You will vegetate and die in here.* (I don't want that). It takes the better part of two days for me to learn this lesson and to teach myself not to move. Which makes it difficult to eat. Actually, it makes it difficult to perform any task.

Like washing. I know most men think that there could be nothing nicer than to be at the receiving end of a lovely, warm sponge bath. Maybe. But only if you enjoy being infantilized.

The art of receiving a bed bath involves a certain degree of difficulty to the extent that it requires the recipient to do nothing – which is sometimes the hardest thing to do. It's all about keeping still, resisting the urge to wiggle (which can be as difficult as fighting a sneeze).

The trick is to let the nursing assistant do his/her work without interference. Do not try to 'help' (get your hands out of the way). Don't try to cover up your bits in what is bound to be an unsuccessful – and false – show of modesty. Let them get on with their work. Stop causing a fuss 'down there'. It will only take longer.

On the other hand, *do* make an effort to lift the dead weight of your lardass. Do not make your healthcare worker struggle unnecessarily.

On the first day of bedridden paralysis my nursing assistant is a plump, square-faced woman whom I think looks German. Perhaps because I expect her to, she helps by shouting monosyllabic commands at me in English. *Lift! Turn! No, right! The other way*! I want to add, *das is gut!,* but hold my tongue. Two weeks later Frédérique and I are laughing and joking up a storm (in French only). Her smile is infectious. Her humour has a confidential, almost intimate quality about it. She makes it seem like we are sharing a private joke.

We but we are not.

*

Sometimes at night I am terrified in the hospital. I panic as my mind spins its wheels, unable to remember how to perform what used to be routine actions. I try to rehearse them in my imagination. How do I make my computer work?

I can't remember my password.

After three days of trying, I remember. Overjoyed, I write it on the bedside table with a nonpermanent felt tip marker. I watch in horror the next day as a nurse's aid, who suspects me of graffiti, wipes it clean. (Not to worry; I will remember it again several days later).

I try to envisage brushing my teeth. The geography of tooth brushing is foreign to me. I attempt to fantasize receiving a blowjob. I can't. I can't get the woman's position and mine in the right order in relation to one another. I cannot figure it out. I cannot visualize it.

It's too difficult for me.

I am suffering from ataxia.

*

(Even if I remembered my password I don't know how to use it.)

*

There are two computers at my house.

One is not password protected. I ask my partner to bring it.

*

In my experience there are two available perspectives on going to the lavatory (taking a shit). The first is to expel it as soon as possible. Why, given a reasonably comfortable and private place to go, delay? The only reason that occurs to me for retaining shit is because its passage would be uncomfortable.

'Painful' would be a good reason.

'Messy' would be the other.

*

Dr Gaillard looks at me silently. Actually, he stares.

I stare back at him.

He has a deep voice which he employs to good effect (its sudden arrival is dramatic, but it also belongs naturally to the silence that precedes it).

Very complicated, he says.

I shrug inside my hospital gown, which slips off my shoulders.

He announces to the room, in English (as if speaking lines in a play): *the case of Monsieur Trombley is very complicated.*

The more he says this, the more certain I am that I will die.

Or not. Another way to view this is medical advisor setting himself up for success.

But, nah. Not buying that.

Actually, I'm not even attempting to sell it.

I trust Dr Gaillard explicitly. He is the expert. I don't believe he is fucking with me. He *my* expert, the one that chance has assigned. The one I am accepting.

So, I'm thinking, let's get to work! And he does.

*

The problem is strokes plus a heart attack (infarctus). Strokes – a few, a lot – no one is sure how many. Heart attacks a few, no one knows just how many or when. Dr Faillon, the female member of the husband-and-wife cardiac team, asks me, *are you sure you don't remember having several heart attacks?* Actually, as a matter of fact, yes, I now remember (having had a few days to think it over). There were four, I think. Around February (but maybe March). One in bed at home in France. Another while visiting friends in

London. And two others in France. All over the course of a month. They were marked by a sharp pain in the back, high up. Yeah, now I remember.

And the strokes? Mmm…. I remember feeling weird in December. I returned from the village shop and was a bit disoriented. I got the break pedal and clutch on my car mixed up. '*Ooops,*' I ejaculated, as I made the same mistake over and over, my car jerking to and fro. My village's sole Christmas decoration winked cheerfully as I struggled with the controls of my automobile.

And then I had problems telling the time. Calculating it, more like. Since moving to southwest France from Nashville I was having the devil of a figuring out the difference between Central Time (as in Illinois, where my employer was based – you don't think I still have a job, do you?) and Brossac. Simple, right? Seven hours behind (except for when it's Daylight Savings Time). Except for when you've had a stroke and don't know it.

And then it gets worse. The time thing. I have lost the ability to generate invoices. I cannot add up. I can't do anything involving sequential.

My boss knows something is wrong and selects an option other than a medical one (and who can blame her – American illness requires fault, fine, blame, guilt.)

She fires me.

*

It is February 2017. Or maybe January. I am having 'visual distortions' (I have given my self-diagnosis its first name). It feels like I am catching a fleeting glimpse of something from the corner of my eye. In February I also have four episodes of double vision. There is no pain during any of this. But there is a worrying sense that each episode might affect my sight permanently.

I decide to take my blood pressure. It is very, very high. I have blood pressure measuring apparatus because a few months previously I'd gone on a heath kick at the local gym. Brought down my blood pressure naturally (with lifestyle changes) to normal. But I since then I'd resumed my old ways (smoking, drinking) without restarting the BP medication. That was silly.

I find a doctor, explain my predicament (BP 187/123 – the doctor is accompanied by an intern whose eyes bug out at the reading). The doctor, a much older man, is nonplussed. Writes me a prescription and orders a blood test. Come back next week, he says.

I after a few days don't think I will make it to next week. I feel horrible.

I have another episode of double vision while working in the garden. Go into my study and struggle to remember the symptoms that brought me to the doctor in the first place. Then I realize I have forgotten the French words for them. I am looking them up and writing them down. My handwriting is tiny and illegible. I do not recognize it as mine. Terrified that I will lose my ability to communicate at any moment, I scribble, in my new miniature hand, 'I am in distress'.

I visit the doctor. I hand him the note. He studies it. Takes my blood pressure and frowns. I'm not going to discuss what should be done next. I pitch him a look that says, *'Hospital. Now.'*

*

'Who is [insert name of woman with whom I have been conducting an affair] *my partner asks?'*

The game is up.

My partner is incredulous.

She had no idea I had been deceiving her.

She is going to leave me.

*

After two weeks I am allowed to sit up in bed while Sabrina holds onto me. She is holding on for safety reasons because sitting up makes me lightheaded. High. Feels like I've just snorted a line of coke. Or had a toke on a strong joint. Or, even, a puff on a cigarette.

Fuck me! That's enough for today.

*

We try again tomorrow and it is better.

Sabrina places her hand in the small of my back and pushes forward, gently. Her cinnamon-coloured skin brushes against mine. She is so soft.

*

Sabrina has caught my wrist tightly in her hand. I look down at her – at the juncture of our bodies, the place where we are connected. She also looks at our connection. Like waiting for a speeding car to pass, she notices it, allows it. Without making eye contact, she resumes helping me sit up.

*

I learn that this sitting position is to be thought of more as a location than an activity. Like *au bord de la mer* (*at the sea side*), *au bord de lit* (*at the edge of the bed,* to *sit up in* bed) signifies a richness and complexity beyond mere verticality.

It means half way to standing up.

Which, I learn, is problematical for me because my brain, greedy for blood, may demand too much of it, leading to a lights out situation in my head (another stroke). Hence the nurses' real concern re dizziness or lightheadedness.

I stand up. It's not so bad. (On day two of standing, the physiotherapist asks me to stand on one leg. I can barely do it. But I couldn't before my stroke. I am not The Karate Kid.)

I'm a little wobbly. I think my legs must be weak from lack of use.

The physiotherapist invites me to go for a walk with her.

I do not like her. I do not like her manner or her execrable English with it's obvious assumption that I can't speak French. When I do, she ignores me. I deal with this by refusing to speak English with her. After two weeks she reverts to using the language in which we are both proficient (no therapy time has been lost since not a great deal of technical skill is required for her to point to her left leg, then her right.)

*

My partner announces the date of her return to the United States.

I plead with her. Not to leave.

Next day she changes her mind.

She will stay.

I am hugely relieved.

I don't deserve her forgiveness. I will spend the rest of my life attempting to be worthy of it.

*

One of the consulting neurologists is a short and (it appears to me) rather smug man. One day, soon after I am allowed to stand and walk, I decide to take a (forbidden? – I don't ask permission) solo promenade. The doctor in question appears from his office. We startle one another, stop, say *bonjour*. I see him check my gait, appraising it professionally. He motions for me to turn around. He does up my hospital gown, which has come unfastened. He nods and sends me on my way.

*

While I am in hospital it is the first round of the French presidential election.

The ultra right wing candidate Marine Le Pen is neck and neck with Emmanuel Macron. Le Pen is a Nazi.

Who is Macron? – you could not be blamed for asking at the time. Centrist. Founder of his own political party, En Marche! (really, a political party with an exclamation mark in its name!).

A terrorist attack on 20 April, two days before the election, threatens to influence the outcome.

Macron wins the first round with 24.01 percent of the vote to Le Pen's 21.3 percent. Talk about close.

Next day I start occupational therapy with Virginie, a young woman in her twenties with a positive and encouraging manner.

'Are you following our election?' she asks while setting out a fiendishly difficult task involving brightly-coloured but tiny pegs in holes.

'Closely'.

She seems surprised. (I am quickly learning that the French really do believe that we English are a nation of uncultured imbeciles. Imagine what she would think if she knew my first nationality was American.) 'And what do you think?'

'What do I think? It is more what I *know*. Voting for a Nazi is simply out of the question.'

Virginie shakes her head as if I don't understand the complexity of the issues.

In the country where Drancy happened.

'There's more to it,' she says, omitting *than* you *can understand.*

She packs our toys away and wheels me back to my room.

*

I reach down and touch my lifeless arm.

No, that's not correct. It isn't lifeless. It's paralyzed.

Same thing? I don't think so. Lifeless means dead. My arm is still alive because there is a bit of feeling left in it. Forty-eight hours after I am struck by the/my stroke ('my' stroke is like a hot potato – *here, you take it, I don't want it!* Claiming ownership of it seems like bad luck.)

But, I think to myself, that's all it is. Just bad luck. Possibly exacerbated by bad lifestyle choices. It could happen to (almost) anyone. I am not going to make too much of a fuss about it. (As I write this I hear dissonant voices saying, *you're just putting on an act.*) Sorry. The fact is, I don't give a fuck. That may be the reason why even though I feel fear in here – and there is plenty to be scared of – I do not express it by curling myself up into a weepy ball.

*

With paralysis it is an excess rather than a lack of feeling that annoys. Paralyzed limbs are heavy! Attempting to lift them takes all your strength and uses all your energy.

But persistence pays off. Even a tiny bit of movement (*did my hand really move just now?*) elicits an elevated pulse and the mad hope that *maybe I will be able to move my arm again (someday) and use my hand!*

If truth be told – and why ever should it not be? – as soon as the first, slightest movement is clocked, you are fine. If you are like me, you *know* this. You *will* get to use your hand again. But, what for, to do what with, is the question that remains to be answered. Maybe not ten pin bowling (though you never know). You might be able to lift your cast iron skillet, but then again you might not. The point is, you probably will recover some use of your limb. Total, pre-stroke use of it? Doubtful, my friend. (Get used to it and quit yer bitchin'. Be glad some poor sod doesn't have to follow you around scraping shit off the back of your legs.)

*

Because you are a reader and I am a writer you may take for granted the existence of the words on this page, but I won't let you.

I already mentioned visual disturbances. Looking about my hospital room the day after my stroke I am confused. And not just about the date. Everything is all jumbled up.

Visually.

Looking at the television is uncomfortable. (During my first month in hospital I do not wear my glasses at all – the first time they've been off my nose since I was thirteen years old. Wearing them does not help.)

When I try to read, I can't. It's all a whirl, a blur.

Writing is out of the question. It's not about legibility. It is muscular, has to do with paralysis. I can't do it. I can't form letters. I CAN'T WRITE.

And, truth be told, I cannot arrange letters in the correct order to form words.

Not being able to write is my worst fear.

But, hold on, let's check all this out, bit by bit. What works and what doesn't.

1. I can't remember anything for more than a few moments.
2. I know what the letters of the alphabet are supposed to look like, I just can't draw them.
3. Reading confuses me. I can I read the first few words of a sentence; then I lose my place and forget where I am.

My first reaction is heart-stopping panic. Then I take a deep breath, try to figure it out. I *can* read, just not very well (or quickly). The fact that I am able to do it gives me hope. Maybe I will grow to do it better.

What about writing? My speech is unaffected. So is my comprehension (I think). I can speak, so I can at least dictate words. Speaking is not the same as writing, but the distinction is too fine for most to acknowledge. I am sensible enough to tell myself to be patient. Writing, the most important of things, will fix itself. Of this I am certain. It is the source of my strength, my confidence.

*

I am keeping Emmanuelle company while she changes the sheets on my bed. She is one of my favourite nurses. She makes small talk easily (funny how people can choose – or not – to talk about nothing with one). She has a wide smile and a vivacious laugh and I look forward to her days on. She is of Caribbean heritage and I have made a mental note to ask her which island, but of course I can't remember to ask her (which is a shame because I have never had the opportunity to say *Guadalupe* out loud and have been longing to). The television newsreader turns his attention to the election. They show Marine Le Pen posing for selfies with factory workers.

'She is racist,' Emmanuelle says. Simply, descriptively, without emphasis.

I agree. She smiles with relief. She has taken a chance, expressing her political opinions in front of a patient.

*

Fucked is what I am.

Spatially, at least. There is an expression, *he doesn't know his arse from his elbow* (*or from hole in the ground*). That's me. I have failed spectacularly at psychoneurological tests designed to unmask an inability to mirror the actions of another. I really don't think I should be allowed out. Spatial perception up the spout.

*

To set the record straight: I was born in upstate NY in 1954. Makes me American. I moved to England when I was nineteen. Lived there without a break until 2003. Married (Englishwoman). Divorced. Married (another Englishwoman). Divorced again, married again. Etc. Became a permanent resident of UK, then citizen. I have dual nationality, US/UK. I lived in France for much of 1999-2003 and recently moved there from Nashville, TN in 2016. That is a nutshell account of me and Europe.

Some basic healthcare facts. (I'm sure everyone knows this stuff, but here it is again for those who spent the last forty years in a coma.) The US spends the highest percentage of GDP on healthcare, 17.1 percent.[*] That is more than double its nearest rival, Switzerland which spends 11.7 percent (France spends 11.5 percent, the UK 9.1 percent). Despite its massive spend, the US ranks only 37th in healthcare outcomes. France is ranked first, while the UK is 18th.[**] The US is the only industrialized country in which healthcare is not a right. A consequence of this is that medical debt is the leading cause of bankruptcy there, affecting more than two million people a year.

The price of my medical treatment in the US would by now have exceeded half a million dollars (and they are not done yet). My bill in France is less than $1,000.

*

To be knocking on heaven's door is no big thing.

Heart attacks are certainly painful, but rank nowhere compared to dental pain. Strokes don't hurt. They are not even scary. They are just boring.

There is an element of the uninterested observer to having a stroke. You watch stuff going on around you. Mostly, strokes make you sleepy.

So, there you are, paralyzed to some degree. Terrified? No. Not at all. Mildly curious (because it is about me, is happening to me? – still, I cannot muster a lot of interest.) Surely, just a little bit scared?

Of what? Dying?

Please. I made friends with my mortality half a century ago.

Death holds no fear for the nonbeliever.

*

In general, women are too necessary to be ill.

Don't have time.

They are too busy.

*

Managing hope and expectations is what it says on the note to I've written to myself to kickstart this morning's work.

Hmm....

Hope is to do with the future. It is our only orientation to the world if we are to avoid despair.

But it can be tricky. If we look forward into the future and the view is unrelentingly grim because our prospects are – as is so often the case for so many – where is hope? The best description of clinical depression I've ever read is 'a sense of hopelessness that disrupts an individual's ability to function.'[*]

You have to have hope to survive a stroke. Not hope that the future will get any better, because it won't (at least if it is measured by the prospect of recovering full, pre-stroke mobility). We are talking about the joy that comes from having a future at all. I think that what I most admire about the stroke survivors I have met is their ability to maintain hope while learning to live with reduced expectations.

*

Avez-vous faire caca?

Have you taken a shit? The nurse shouts the question into my hospital room while cheerfully making herself busy emptying my hand-held urinal (*pistolet*). She repeats, louder, *avez-vous faire caca?*

Caca is more accurately translated as *poo*.

Poo.

It is, at best, a child's colloquialism. It is infantile.

But there is so much about hospital that can be viewed as 'infantile' (or infantilizing). Maybe these things are more accurately understood as relating to the other end of life's timeline; instead of learning, gaining control, we are losing it, or learning to let go.

Which is just a big pile of poo.

The simple fact is, the French are obsessed with their bowels.

Watch TV from a French hospital bed for several weeks and you will discover this from the number of laxative adverts.

Dulcolax ads are best. They feature a blonde woman of the young mother type who is deliciously mignon. Her facial expression indicates her discomfort down there. The advertisement suggests that the medicine acts quickly. There is a very nice shot of her tummy. Then she twirls in her little house dress to indicate that all is well.

There is no way that her shit stinks.

The nurse slips me a glyercine-like dose of laxative.

*

I had an accident in the parking lot.

I had an accident in my trousers.

I had a cerebrovascular accident.

They call a cerebrovascular accident a 'stroke'. Which is odd, because English is such a rich language and you'd think we could come up with something more precise than the same word we use for petting a cat, having a wank or measuring the time as tolled by a clock. (Nowadays 'they' increasingly say 'brain attack'). Truth be told, 'stroke' is a lexicographer's dream (or nightmare) come true. It can mean the mark made by a pen or brush (or the movement of a sword). Hitting a ball while playing a sport (strokes in cricket, tennis, golf, swimming). Corporal punishment (strokes of lash or paddle. A sudden (generally positive and often sudden) turn of events (a stroke of luck/genius, several problems solved at a stroke). He is a lazy boy, hasn't done a stroke of work all day. Etc.

A 'stroke'. In our usage it is a medical emergency in which part of the brain is deprived of oxygen (which always has bad consequences). One way of describing it is 'the sudden death of brain cells due to lack of oxygen, caused by blockage of blood flow or rupture of an artery to the brain.'* Or, a 'neurological deficit of cerebrovascular cause that persists beyond 24 hours or is interrupted by death within 24 hours.'**

It is amusing (and quite accurate) to view stroke as an 'accident' – 'an unfortunate incident that happens unexpectedly and unintentionally, typically resulting in damage or injury.'*** There is also a sense in which this 'accident' is preventable (as unwanted pregnancy can be avoided by the use of contraception, so the chances of stroke can be reduced by choosing not to smoke).

I mostly think of a stroke as my brain exploding.

*

Of the nurses I perhaps like Claire the best.

She is not pretty and her face looks like it is designed to wear those sixties spectacles that go up in little points. (But she doesn't wear them). Despite her cheerfulness she seems perpetually careworn. Preoccupied.

While she changes my sheets (I love that the nurses have time to chat while taking care of me)

Claire talks about her family. Shares her worries. She has a son who is sixteen and a daughter who is fourteen. She is worried that they don't read enough.

She talks about 'the service' (the French nursing service) in a way I've heard other nurses refer to their employer: with a mixture of love and respect, as if it is an honour to serve. Keep in mind that this is a faceless bureaucracy. Yet it generates passionate loyalty.

Claire is married to a soldier. Our conversation turns to war. She talks about her experience of it, and how she is morally obliged to extend nursing care to any human being, friend or foe. And to treat them the same. Listening to her talk I know she has done this.

*

Soon after Claire leaves the cleaner comes to visit, as she does every day. There are four cleaners on my ward and they are all of a type. They all have a veneer of tentativeness about entering your room. But it is a façade. Because they are the cleaner, they have a right to enter and, as they hover in the doorway, they are about to exercise it. So that whole tentative thing is…what it is.

Cleaners the world over have traits in common. They like to have a good look around. My ones have this in common: they are quiet as mice (not all cleaners are).

The are also very, very good at cleaning. (Not all cleaners are).

*

As soon as they installed an IV and got me admitted they scanned my brain. This was within minutes of arriving in hospital. Those first minutes were a bit confusing. One thing, though, was certain: I was now well and truly *in* hospital. When would I get *out*? is a question I did not think to ask myself or anyone else. If, at that moment, I knew the answer I would be terrified; would think something was the matter with me. Odd how I knew not to ask.

Brain scan. All very well. Trips casually off the tongue.

But what does it mean? I don't know, really. I suppose I could look it up. I'm not sure what the point would be, as I'd soon forget it. The main thing is, it doesn't interest me. I can't be bothered.

I just don't give a fuck.

Does that sound as though I don't care (about myself)? I think I do care about myself. Maybe I just have a funny way of showing it. To be honest, I can't get interested in the detail of it. It is technical stuff about which I know nothing.

Anyway, I am in no fit state to be a student of anything.

But, am I not just a little bit curious?

No I am not. Now fuck off.

*

On another day (which day, I have no idea) they bring me down for an MRI. I am getting used to my trips in the lift. It is an odd experience, viewing the world from on your back, being wheeled on a gurney. There is a lot of colliding with walls. It's noisy. (Later, when I am able to walk and my topographical knowledge expands, I will notice the that the mortuary in located in the basement.)

The MRI is a noisy affair. When the machine has finished its clanking, banging and buzzing the technicians wheel me out of the room. They leave me in an antechamber to one side.

I have to pee. I eventually attract someone's attention.

I guess it's true the world over, shift changes are a bitch.

*

I have two echocardiograms (ultrasounds of the heart). The first is performed by a pleasant young man. A week later Dr Faillon (the female half of the cardio duo) decides she would like to perform a second one. I cannot remember why, only that she seems pleased (in a cautious way) with the result. Her satisfied smile feels like the best news ever and cheers me up no end.

*

One afternoon I am wheeled down for a transesophageal echocardiography. This test involves swallowing a camera. It is too foul to describe in detail.

*

Vous êtes grand, monsieur!

I'm tall.

All the nurses say so.

In French hospitals it is almost always the first thing people say to me: 'you're tall'. Except when they are shouting *what is your name* at me or demanding to know the date (whatever happened to *please?*)

At six feet and two inches tall I am 'grand' by French standards. Or French hospital beds are shorter, which is what I suspect.

A nurse who just said I am 'grand' calls her mate over to show her. *Ooh, vous êtes grand, monsieur*, her friend remarks.

'How tall *are* you,' the friend asks. I shrug my shoulders. That question is as about as likely to elicit a correct answer as *what time is it*, or *what is today's date*? 'How much do you weigh?' I smile. They will get it eventually: I have no idea what any of these answers might be. The questions are accompanied by an equal lack of interest on my part.

Next thing I know I am being wheeled into a room which contains a hoist. A winch. It looks like you would use it to lift very heavy people (or a car engine).

It is scales. They are going to weigh me.

Next they will measure me. See how long I am. (They cannot measure my height standing up for the same reason they can't weigh me while standing, because it could cause blood to drain from my head – potential lights out situation).

So they measure my length. These are excellent nurses. They know to have a laugh.

*

After a week the paralysis affecting my right arm lessens. Every morning Dr Gaillard and a nurse come to inspect it. The nurses are first to mark my progress because they are first to say 'raise your arms' during their morning examination.

The first couple of days are very disappointing. I can get my arm to lift a bit but I can't get it to stay there. It is a cause for celebration when I can hold it up for a few seconds (three months after The Accident I can hold it up for 'a long time', but it wobbles).

As my arm grows stronger by tiny increments I take a childlike delight in flexing my muscles, such as the are, Popeye-style for Dr Gaillard.

Each morning the nurse, then Dr Gaillard, tests my arm's resistance. I am thrilled that I can mark forward progress every day by this method. (Progress still continues after three months, though the advances are less dramatic).

As I grow more confident in my eating habits I fear I also become messier. The more I recover the ability to leverage food with knife and fork while cutting it, the greater the force with which it might fly off the plate. (During the days when I was relearning to feed myself I apologized to one of the nursing assistants who told me, 'don't worry, it's easier this way'. Which translates as, 'don't worry, it's quicker and less messy for us to feed you than for you to feed yourself, chucking food about the way you do.')

You learn to time your chewing and swallowing to suit the rhythm of your feeder. One of them feeds me so fast it feels like I am training for that world hot dog eating championship on

Coney Island. It is nothing like how I imagined my mother's slow spoon feeding of me as an infant.

*

It amazes me how doctors and nurses can work all day around sick people and generally avoid falling ill themselves. They place themselves in the midst of contagion yet avoid disease. If they are lucky.

They are courageous.

It is not only disease that doctors and nurses often don't succumb to: it is also disgust. Perhaps they have a mechanism that stifles their gag reflex. Perhaps their noses just don't smell foul odours. They certainly do a good job of ignoring them if they do.

Somehow they are not scathed by stuff that makes ordinary people vomit.

I guess diseases cannot be entirely avoided since they are there to be caught and luck (or the lack of it) would seem to play a part; but disgust is visceral (and would appear to be non-negotiable). Additionally, disgust can have a moral component, an element of disapproval.

It can be a judgment.

For instance, shit, on its own, can be disgusting. But shit, rubbed in, can be repulsive because we disapprove of it (we disapprove of the *intentional* quality of the act of rubbing it in; it is some one's fault, there is a candidate for blame).

Perhaps this is why it is essential that an unexpected bowel movement be regarded as an 'accident'. It must be stripped of intentionality.

*

No one courts constipation. But I can attest to the motivation for avoiding bowel movements in hospital. No one, I think, looks forward to using the bedpan. The main reason is because when it's time to shit in the bedpan we are no longer talking about small, firm pebbles. No. We are talking about massive, shapeless, squidgy poos that have been building up for a while. The kind that make a mess. A stinky mess. The kind that sticks to the back of your legs. That is why hospital patients put off evacuating their bowels for as long as possible. Because, as tolerant and seemingly immune as nurses are to grossness, we don't want to test them.

Footnotes

* WHO, 13 February 2017. http://www.who.int/gho/health_financing/total_expenditure/en/

** WHO, 2000. https://producaoindustrialblog.com/2017/01/15/world-health-organizations-ranking-ofthe-worlds-health-systems/

* Cleo Hutton, *After a Stroke: 300 Tips for Making Life Easier.*

* medicinenet.com.

** World Health Organisation (1978). *Cerebrovascular Disorders (Offset Publications).* Geneva: World Health Organization. ISBN 92-4-170043-2. OCLC 4757533.

*** *OED.*

Patients

Jean-Luc is the only male day shift nurse. He has what seems a Russian appearance and is very quiet. He pitches up and informs me that we are going to change rooms. Now.

I guess my condition has been upgraded. I am leaving intensive care.

Seconds later a nursing assistant arrives and starts loading my stuff into what appears to be a bin liner. They pump the brake on my hospital bed and off we go.

After much banging and colliding with walls I am *installé* in my new room. The journey takes only a few seconds. My new room (shared, I notice, but I appear to be its sole occupant at present) is just a few doors down from my old one.

The telly is permanently set to mute. Makes sense. Privacy.

After ten minutes or so I hear voices in the hall and a man who is clearly my new roommate is wheeled in. We nod and then I hear him explain to the orderly that he has been promised a private room. The orderly says he will look into it and leaves.

*

My roommate is older than me.

We nod at one another again. Gruffly.

He opens a bag of snacks and starts munching.

Astrid is the second prettiest nurse after Renée. I wouldn't call her gruff, but she is certainly businesslike. She comes to do our blood pressure. My roommate is monosyllabic throughout the encounter with Astrid. When she's done with him it's my turn. We joke and banter. She slips the cuff on and keeps up her chatter. Says 'later' and exits the room leaving traces of good cheer.

*

Roommate's wife arrives. We say hello. Seems like a nice woman. Worry is written on her face.

The thing about hospital beds is that you can draw the curtain separating them, but you can't make the room soundproof. And, the more people try to be quiet by whispering, the louder they are. I learn that my roommate owns a couscous restaurant (I did not not have him pegged as a *pied noir*), and that business could be better. Listening to him talk to his wife I find him likable. She leaves after about four hours.

He gets up to *faire pipi* and demonstrates a little more warmth as he must pass by my bed on his way to and from the toilet. I ask if they have arranged his private room yet. He is a little surprised and I think a lot pleased. He smiles and says, 'no'.

Dinner arrives. I am still paralyzed and need help cutting my food and removing yoghurt tops (I can put the food in my cake hole unassisted). I've got company now, so a bit more modesty is in order. I ask the nurse to help me pull my gown across my backside. I am sitting up in bed slopping food all down my front. The restaurant owner is a quiet eater. When the nursing assistant comes to take his tray she knows to make a joky remark for him about hospital food. It is successful. They laugh.

Good.

The nursing assistant comes back, smiling, to clean up my mess.

*

Haven't shared a room with another bloke for donkeys.

The sights, smells and sounds of male intimate proximity are a little startling to me. It's been years since I've encountered (actually, been confronted with) them. Smelling the shit of another man. Seeing (glimpsing) his nakedness. Hearing his bodily functions. Oddly, perhaps, I find the odour of toothpaste most invasive of my privacy.

The French are generally in good physical condition, ie not obese. This is my first time observing another stroke patient. I think my roommate's stroke must have been what they call a 'mild' one as he's up and about and they are diacussing sending him home after only 48 hours. We eye each other up. I do not think he is especially pleased to notice that he is less fucked than I am.

I bet he's relieved, though.

He's not paralyzed. At least, not so you'd notice.

My roommate and I are a little more talkative now. We agree to ask the nurse to lower the shutter and darken the room. It is eight p.m. Time for first attempt at sleep in shared room.

I am thinking about today. I think about the bigger picture of today. I am in a French hospital. Because I am a citizen of Europe I am entitled to French medical treatment. I am being cared for by French nurses who are lovelier than you can imagine. The nurses are employees of a state founded on ideas of freedom and equality. And yes, brotherhood. Not only that, the French health service is rated the best in the world by independent observers who know about this stuff.

I count myself fortunate.

(And half a million dollars of healthcare is not nothing).

*

A stroke is catastrophic.

It impacts a person's earning capacity.

It wasn't too many hours after my stroke that I realized my money-earning days might be behind me. It also was not too many hours before I realized there was nothing I could do about it.

Soon after he wakes my neighbour engages me in a conversation about his restaurant. He is worried that it will fail on account of his stroke. And then, in almost the same breath, he says 'if it does, it does'. I find this interesting, my roommate's almost instant acceptance of what has happened to him. I experienced the same thing. I wonder if it goes with the territory.

My roommate and I have established a distant cordiality. I like him.

After lunch his wife visits again. She offers a respectful greeting then draws the curtain. They discuss money.

An hour later, my roommate's son and daughter arrive. They, too, are working class. The son's costume (track suit), jewellery (gold chain) and accent testify to this. They are a lovely family. The teen daughter is shy. After they leave, my roommate tells me that she is studying English and Mandarin at lycée.

The two days later he is released from hospital. I have enjoyed this accidental collision of our paths (though not the circumstances).

He wishes me *bon courage*.

I wish him the same.

*

Later that day I get a new roommate.

He is a tiny fellow. Spry. Fit.

He has a black eye (from a fall?)

He is very particular about his belongings. He makes a handwritten inventory of the contents of his suitcase using the white board and marker provided in each room.

He unpacks carefully and sits on the bed. Perhaps he is not staying.

We nod at one another.

My new roommate is, I realize upon closer inspection, older than he looks. (The skin on his face is taut, giving the appearance of youth).

He is restless. He cannot stop fiddling with his stuff. He is unrelentingly noisy in the way that deeply annoying people are when they are ostentatiously (and aggressively) making a show of trying not to be.

I have grown accustomed to weeks of quiet. This man is disrupting it.

Of course, I feel sorry for the old fucker.

Ça va? I say to him.

*

A consultant arrives to examine my roommate (whose name is Henri). The curtain is drawn but visual privacy is the only sort afforded. I learn that he has had an accident. He has taken a tumble in the street. (But has obviously stopped at home first, hence the suitcase). Has he had a stroke? I don't think so. He is confused, doesn't know where he is. He is surprised to learn he is not in Bordeaux. He attempts strenuously to dispute this fact. Lets the doctor know that he thinks a trick is being played on him and that he is wise to it.

He doesn't know what day or month it is (but neither do I).

He says he has two children, a son and a daughter. I do not overhear mention of a wife.

He tells the doctor he is diabetic. (When the nurse later asks him if he is, he replies that he is not).

The consultant leaves and Henri continues to make himself busy in the room. Renée comes in to take our blood pressure. Henri talks the hind leg off a donkey. She politely listens while he explains to her that he will be leaving soon. She gives me the most delicious smile.

Henri meticulously packs his suitcase then uses the loo. He leaves the room. A nurse him fetches him and brings him back. He sits on the bed for half an hour, gets up, leaves again.

A nurse returns with him a minute later.

*

It is bedtime.

There is a loud and prolonged sound of rustling bedclothes from next door. The nursing assistant comes in to check on us and say goodnight. Henri has got the bedclothes off the bed and in a terrible tangle. She shouts at him in a good-natured way, scolds him, remakes his bed and puts him back in it.

I am awakened in the middle of the night by the noise of Henri trying to be quiet. The room is moonlit (I neglected to get a lights management agreement in place before bedtime). I can make out the shadowy figure of Henri leaving.

Christ. Can't have the old bloke doing a runner in the middle of the night.

I press the alarm button.

When the nurse comes I explain what has happened.

She returns with Henri in tow.

He gives me a dirty look.

The nurse, taken aback at the cheek of Henri's attempted escape, thanks me.

*

The next forty-eight hours are sleepless as Henri repeatedly attempts to do a runner.

I reflect that, if this were America he would have been restrained hours ago. The scene would likely escalate; turn violent as this tiny wisp of a man was assaulted by 'security'. Make no mistake, the guy is as annoying as fuck. But that doesn't mean (at least in France) that we deprive him of his rights (even though my private thoughts include strangling him). He is annoying as fuck.

The day shift nurse comes in and whispers an apology, promises to get Henri moved to another room. (I doubt this will happen – if there were anywhere else for him to go he would be there).

I am fucking exhausted.

The second night with Henri is worse. He makes three breakout attempts. This is getting tedious. The first couple of times I think I am helping the staff look after an old bloke. Third time I am pissed off.

Two nights without sleep, my ears alert to every sound. Renée comes to tuck us in and I hear her angrily rebuke Henri. He is trying to explain himself and I overhear him say *bêtise* (literally *stupidity*). I know right away that my roommate has been sexually offensive. Renée is not wearing her usual smile as she stomps out of the room. I spend a third sleepless night listening to Henri hover at the edge of his bed in between unauthorized exit attempts. On his third try, I think fuck it and leave him to it. The nurse brings him back.

When the day shift comes on I will make a complaint.

There is no need. They come for Henri's stuff. While I am out for a walk in the corridor I see that he has been placed in a room that locks from the outside. He is kept in there for three days. And then he is gone.

No one came to visit Henri.

*

They waste no time in replacing Henri the Escape Artist. My new roommate is Monsieur Morel.

I find it hard to form as assessment of M Morel since he is asleep nearly the whole time. When the doctor comes in to have a look at him I learn that he can raise his arms in front of him (no paralysis, then). But his speech is affected. It is very 'thick'. I can tell that he is intentionally keeping the volume down, as if he is both surprised and repelled by the sounds coming from himself.

It is interesting to me, the variety of ways in which stroke manifests itself. The varying severity of it. I am very glad that my speech isn't affected.

But then I think, would I trade the use of my right arm for a speech defect? (I don't know that I would.) I am aware that we tend to discount the intellectual ability of someone who struggles with speech even though their difficulty may be no indicator of mental impairment.

Soon after lunch Mme Morel arrives. A brusque woman, she sweeps into the room and after a perfunctory greeting draws the curtain and proceeds with her agenda. She wants to know *how he* (her husband) *is*. (I can answer that one: *he's been better*!) She gives him family news and then mentions (for the first of a hundred times) the name of a doctor. His name is uttered with reverence. Ah. This is the myth of *my* doctor. The one you may well feel more comfortable with because you think you know him, but who is very unlikely to possess the particular skills and experience of the state-provided consultant who is a specialist re strokes that your husband has just had the good fortune to be examined by. *Doctor X says this, Doctor X says that, Doctor X thinks....*

Mme Morel has been reading about how to help her stroke patient. One of the ways of preserving his dignity and indicating there is someone at home who cares is to dress him in fresh pyjamas daily. (Trouble is, pyjamas are not as practical as a hospital gown when clearing shit from behind the patient.)

She has been learning about the importance for her husband of knowing what day it is. (Poor M Morel hasn't got a clue.) She reads aloud from simple comprehension tests which he is unable to answer. I admire both of them: him for his patience in not losing it with her, and her for her persistence.

Late afternoon and all is quiet next door. Minutes pass without a sound. I look over. I can see, beneath the curtain, that M Morel is sitting up in his chair with his legs spread. Mrs Morel is standing between them.

They don't make a sound.

*

Mme Morel is dogged in pursuit of her husband's recovery.

After only two days his speech has improved dramatically.

She gathers his soiled pyjamas, makes a face, exchanges them for new ones.

Their son comes to visit. He is a young man (a regional sales manager I am guessing). He is helping his mother ensure that his father is seen by 'his' doctor in addition to the consultant neurologist assigned to his case.

Sometimes the son is accompanied by his wife.

When the son leaves, M and Mme Morel again go all quiet while embracing. I look away.

Mme Morel resumes her patient but insistent interrogation of her husband: what day is it? What is the time? Establishing the external realities. The objective stuff that everyone can agree on.

*

It is the second round of the French presidential election. The nation must decide between the fascist Marine Le Pen and the moderate Emmanuel Macron. M Morel pays close attention. He watches with his wife and son. I cannot tell from his remarks which candidate he favours. Mostly he shakes his head at the turnout (forty-two percent, a record low). I think that, in the end, the Morels are satisfied with Macron's victory.

Next day I sense another victory vibe from next door. Mme Morel, who has been lobbying for her husband's release (or is it transfer?), has been successful. There is a brief traffic jam in my room as nurses, the Morels and the ambulance driver gather.

Mme Morel bids me *adieu* and they are off.

*

One of the consultant neurologists enters accompanied by a young man dressed in skinny jeans.

I divine from their conversation that my new roommate is a medic. I hear the consultant refer to me as a writer (but he doesn't acknowledge me). The consultant leaves and Fabien introduces himself.

Fabien is in hospital overnight. Tonight is observation, tomorrow intravenous administration of drugs. Fabien has an exceedingly rare and incurable genetic disease for which he is receiving experimental treatment. (I cannot remember the name of his disease.) This is an emergency visit.

Fabien asks me about my work and listens thoughtfully and carefully to my reply. We chat at length. This is my first encounter with anyone younger than myself in hospital, except for nurses.

Fabien may be the youngest person in the room but he exudes, in the absence of consultants or other senior medical staff, a natural sense of command. (He expects his instructions to nurses to be followed as if they are orders, which they are). Astrid is in the room and she watches while Fabien inspects the functioning of the drip. He arrived between lunch and dinner and asks for two containers of apple sauce. Astrid leaves then reappears a few moments later with the young doctor's snack.

*

Fabien is a chick magnet.

He's got Renée and Astrid in the room, both of them slightly breathless (a word that takes much longer to say in French, but which is possessed of a certain *je ne sais quoi* this way – *à bout de souffle*).

It is morning. Renée, Astrid and Fabien are futzing with the intravenous drip mechanism. Fabien dismisses the nurses with the slightest nod of his head. He reaches for his computer and wheels his intravenous apparatus alongside my bed, asks for permission to sit.

'I hacked your medical records last night so we can look at your brain scan,' he says.

'Sweet'.

*

Fabien gets my brain up on the screen and starts poking around. He uses his finger as a pointer.

'See this dark area? These cells are all dead. Your brain is dead here.' He jabs at the screen.

'Alright.'

'We have a good surgeon'.

'Okay.'

'We do this stuff every day, here.'

I thank Fabian for hacking my computer. I am immensely cheered up.

*

Fabien returns to his bed to receive intravenously-administered drugs designed to save his life. Astrid works the mechanism as Fabien observes. When they are both satisfied the thing is working she asks if he is comfortable, has everything he needs.

I'm not chopped liver to her now, but near enough.

Fabien continues our conversation as though it has not been interrupted. 'Of course, we'll have to monitor your blood pressure every day and you will have to have your blood tested every week for the rest of your life. But it's a small price to pay.'

I think so.

I did not realize how attached I am to living until The Accident.

*

I had wondered if looking at my brain scan might be weird in the way that catching a glimpse of my paralyzed arm is, but no.

I have no sense of alienation. It's just a picture of my brain.

Though I suppose it is odd, observing the thing you use for looking at stuff. And not just looking, but imagining, too. The thing that generates ideas.

It is certainly odd to look at it critically, to *read* it, to understand that this part is living while that part is dead. It is strange to sit in judgment of your own brain, actually to be able to have the thought about it, *this part is dead.*

*

Fabien is a hipster and for that reason alone I am inclined to dismiss him as a serious person.

But that would be completely wrong, and I know it. Instead, I think, *gosh, he must have a strong and focused mind to withstand the annoying music that must be leaking out of those noise-cancelling headphones.*

Fabien is a good bloke. He loves football (Paris Saint-Germain). He goes drinking with his professors.

Just before Fabien's treatment is concluded his girlfriend arrives. She is petite, pretty and charming.

This episode in our lives has reached its conclusion.

We shake hands.

I hope he will be okay.

*

My new roommate is Paul.

He is short and stocky and smells of cologne.

His stroke has not paralyzed him, but it has weakened his right leg. He can't walk without holding on.

He is chatty, good-natured. He is up and down frequently for the loo. He smiles painfully each time he limps by.

'*Ça va?*' he asks.

We spend four days together. We talk about *reeducation* as the French rather sinisterly call it (in English we say *rehabilitation*). We are both candidates for it. This is something to look forward to. It is like graduating from the stroke ward. It is like being sent to a halfway house prior to release from prison (I've not dwelt much on how similar hospital and prison are – but they are).

*

Paul walks past on his way to the loo; I see him wobble and then fall.

He is not bleeding, does not seem to have injured himself in that way. I am struggling to sit up in bed, get to his aid, but my paralysis won't let me.

I feel helpless because I can't help my friend. He has gone down like the proverbial ton of bricks. It was a sickening sound, a soft thud. It sounded incredibly painful, and I think it was. I worry that Paul has sprained or broken something.

I reach for the alarm button and press it, making sure that the flashing light is on. I tell Paul to stay put and wait for help. (Don't want him to aggravate a potential fracture.) I mean, how long can it take for someone to respond…?

Paul ignores me and struggles on the floor like a drowning man. I am imploring him to keep still and wait for help. (*How* long can it take them to respond?) Paul pays me no mind whatsoever and continues his futile swim across the floor to the entrance to the bathroom. On his belly.

Paul shoots me a look that says, why don't you stop acting like a cripple and get out of bed and help me? I reply with a look that says, I'm not acting like a cripple, I am a fucking cripple!

A nurse's aide, and then a nurse arrive and help Paul to his feet.

He gives me a rueful, apologetic smile. I ask him if he is okay. He is.

Nasty business, this stroke stuff.

*

Arrr!

Pirate noises are coming from a room on the far end of the intensive care ward.

Arrr!

They are very, very loud pirate noises. They are regular and have been going on for around a week.

They are intensely distressing to me. I don't think they are pirate noises at all. I think they are cries of anguish – of an elderly man in terrible agony.

*

It is Friday and my partner and I have agreed to every other day visits (she finds daily visits too tiring).

It is now Saturday lunchtime and she is not here.

It now Sunday. Something is wrong.

I deserve whatever I get for my wrongdoing, but I am desperately worried.

Claire gently suggests that maybe I have misunderstood the arrangements. It is possible, but I know I haven't.

I imagine her car overturned on a lonely country road.

I cannot remember how to use the telephone, much less plan and execute an action involving one. I ask the assistant to look up my home telephone number on my admissions record and dial it. She does. No reply.

And again, later on.

After several more hours of worry I explain my fear to the male nurse, Jean-Luc. He asks if I would like him to alert the gendarmes. I say that I would. An hour later the police return Jean-Luc's call. I brace myself for the worst. I ask if my partner is okay. The policeman says, 'yes'. I express relief and ask if she is there. I hear him ask if she wishes to speak with me, and then she comes on the line: 'what's up?'

She visits one more time before telling me she will be leaving. I ask about her changing her mind about leaving.

'I lied,' she explains.

*

Upon liberation from intensive care I discover that finding my balance is a little tricky.

But I soon get the hang of verticality.

Within days of being admitted to intensive care I had been looking forward to getting out of hospital. But first I needed to learn patience.

I now have a goal. It's not release from hospital (this is far too serious a crisis, I am far too ill – though I don't fully realize it at first– to even think about going home) but rather transfer to *reeducation* (rehab, physical therapy). This becomes paramount. The next step.

But the next step to what? The concept of 'full health' (as in 'return to') does not occur to me. Why? Because it does not seem possible. All I can imagine is what is in front of me, what is real. And, for the time being, what is real is stroky stuff and its consequences.

A key consequence of The Accident is having to take a selection of life-preserving drugs. (But not as many as you might imagine. You think of really ill people having to swallow fistsful of tablets daily; I only need to take six.) They are:

- Perindopril 4 mg. An ACE (angiotensin-converting-enzyme) inhibitor to control high blood pressure and prevent stroke and heart failure. Increased to 8 mg in November.
- Bisoprolol 1.25 mg. A beta blocker to lower the risk of a second heart attack and to treat high blood pressure and arrhythmias.
- Previscan 20 mg. Also known as fluindione it is an anticoagulant that works by inhibiting vitamin K.
- Pantoprazole 40 mg. For treatment of erosive esophagitis associated with gastroesophageal reflux disease.

- Atorvastatine 40 mg. A statin (cholesterol-reducing drug) that helps prevent cardiovascular disease.
- Kardegic 75 mg. Aspirin, aids in prevention of stroke and heart attack.

Only a few decades ago, the medical and surgical interventions that saved my life had yet to be invented.

Science.

*

For two weeks Dr Gaillard has been talking to me about 'Reeducation).

The reeducation hospital is in Fignac, a town with a population of less than 5,000. Despite its relatively small size it has a hospital with a dedicated residential and outpatient stroke reeducation facility.

Dr Gaillard and I speak of Fignac with a kind of awe, as if it is a promised land. Which it is, really. For Dr Gaillard, Fignac is a milestone: it represents the successful conclusion of my treatment under his care. It is a kind of ceremonial (and practical) handing over of my case to the next stage in the healing process. For me it is a sort of passing out ceremony, a promotion to the next level.

If these are not reasons enough to look forward to my 'transfer' (as it is called), I could add the 'let me out of this fucking place' factor. I have been detained here for five weeks and I would really like to go home.

*

I feel lightheaded.

The nurse calls for the doctor. It is night shift and I have to wait a while.

The doctor examines me, takes my pillows away and tells me to lie back with my feet slightly raised. An hour goes by and I haven't moved. I ring for the nurse. She gives permission to put a pillow under my head. I hate it when my feet are higher than my head.

*

When Dr Gaillard comes on his morning rounds and frowns upon hearing from the nurse of last night's dizziness and tells me I must wait one more week for my transfer to Fignac.

I have grown used to setbacks and delays.

So I resign myself to another week in here.

Okay.

That is, if I don't have any more 'dizzy spells'. If I don't have another 'funny turn'. If I don't 'come over all peculiar' again.

*

Finally, it is really here: transfer day.

Tonight, all will be different. I will go to sleep in the 'reeducation' hospital on Fignac.

But it is morning and I am in the big hospital and Sabrina brings my breakfast: café au lait, bread, butter, jam.

She gives me a big smile, then says, cheerily, 'good morning'.

I am stunned. 'I didn't know you speak English!'

'I do,' she tells me. And then smiles again. 'But you speak French good so I don't need to speak English'.

I don't speak French that well, but it is a nice compliment. (Fucking hell, she speaks English!)

*

Last night's roommate was Eric, in for two nights (heart test).

Eric is a fussbudget. He uses many words when a nod of the head will do. But he seems a nice man (despite smelling of toothpaste).

Eric is preoccupied with what Americans call 'paperwork' (a term used to take the fear out of serious stuff like court orders and last wills and testaments, but which can just as easily apply to an order for scented candles from Amazon). He peers at his multipage document that wants multiple signatures on multiple pages.

Eric's wife is like me. She is used to waffle, to idle chatter, to tongue-wagging for its own sake. She smiles at me without pretending to listen to him.

They are ready to go. Eric has taken an age to pack his pyjamas (even if I had someone at home I would opt for hospital issue with the convenient opening at the rear).

They bid me farewell and good luck.

*

Dr Gaillard hovers in the doorway. He and Renée are checking last-minute stuff to do with my transfer.

The ambulance is booked for two-thirty this afternoon.

Renée looks over at me and smiles. 'Ça va?' she enquires, pleasantly.

Of all the new faces to which I've grown accustomed I will miss hers the most.

Dr Gaillard fully enters the room. He stands there, musing.

I would like to hug him.

'You are very brave,' he says, as if I had singlehandedly taken out a German machine gun emplacement. 'Au revoir,' he says. 'Bon courage.'

And is gone.

I am sat in my street clothes for the first time in five weeks. Renée smiles at me some more.

I imagine how it will be when I say goodbye to her in a few hours.

*

When I was first checked into hospital there was a lot of confusion over the 'paperwork'.

My partner gave the woman my European Health Insurance Card and my UK passport – the correct (and only) documents required. (Dr Gaillard was eventually consulted and was indignant on my behalf, *of course they are the only documents you need,* YOU ARE A EUROPEAN CITIZEN!) The administrator incorrectly disputed this for more than a week, harassing my partner at home (bringing a nascent using-the-phone-to-speak-French phobia to the fore).

At two-thirty the ambulance man arrives. A nurse back at the desk and out of view has already signed the *ordonnance* for my release. I look to see if any of my nurses are around. They are all busy. I am wheeled into the lift and that is that.

*

I pass into the glare of the public part of the hospital. The taxi driver is *au fait* with the hospital discharge procedure and brings me to the right place. The woman behind the desk takes my details, prints an invoice and hands it to me. I have been here for thirty-three days and the cost, including all scans, tests, etc is €594.00.*

*

I am oddly nervous, tentative as I exit the hospital.

There is nothing new involved in this, yet it is strangely unfamiliar to me. I have a memory of doing this (walking in a parking lot, getting into a car, etc) but it is different now. All of it. It is not just the added concentration required for the use of a waking stick, but the whole 'what goes where' in relation to my feet, hands. My entire body seems to be in the way. This is more difficult than I remember.

*

Am I behaving correctly or do I come across as a fucking prima donna?

After five weeks I hospital, three of them spent virtually motionless, I have got used to not doing things for myself. In fact, I have got used to being shouted at, scolded, for attempting to do stuff by myself. Guilt at this behaviour soon enough turned to resignation. Giving in to these new no-self-help rules was not easy, but following them was easier than enduring the shouty consequences. (I hated making the nurses angry, even when their anger had an ironical tinge to it. I knew that the irony concealed a very real edge.)

So, when I stand to one side to allow the taxi driver to open the door for me and he just climbs into his car, shuts the door and waits, I'm like *what the fuck?*

Footnote

* $701.74 or £537.68 on 8 August 2017.

At a Stroke: Diary of a Recovery

Reededucation

So this is what 'normal' must be like.

Sitting in the back of a cab, going somewhere.

To be honest, I liked the little world of the hospital ward better. I liked the nurses. I liked the doctors. The nurse's aides. The cleaners. All of them. I miss it already.

The world outside lacks colour. It lacks vitality.

I like hospital better.

*

We arrive at the reeducation centre but not before getting hopelessly lost less than 500 metres from the front door.

It starts to rain halfway through the thirty-minute journey between the two hospitals and is now pouring. The cab driver goes in to check that the entrance is the right one. Yes it is. But is a long way from the front door. He opens the boot with his remote control and stands there. I also stand there, in the rain, and wait for him to help me with my bags, computer, walking stick.

*

There is nothing I dislike more than stupid people who reinforce class stereotypes.

I am using 'class' here in the mathematical (pure) sense as opposed to the pejorative one denoting social rank. And I am referring to that class of persons employed as hospital administrators in France who have special responsibility for admissions.

I present myself to the admissions person. I hand her my passport (proof of identity) and European Health Insurance Card (proves I am entitled to medical care in France, equivalent of Carte Vitale). She makes a face. Rejects my documents. Asks for 'carte d'identité et Carte Vitale'. I explain what she is paid to know, that they are the same (but in foreign). She won't have it. I explain that I am done wasting time and that she may accept my documentation at her leisure.

The taxi driver is stunned (as in, 'blimey, mate, you can't do that').

I proceed to the ward.

And I am fucking exhausted.

*

Not for the first time I remind myself what a good thing it is that I do not give a fuck.

I head upstairs to the rehabilitation ward where I am greeted by a compact and attractive (if unsmiling) nurse called Virginie. Driver has her sign *ordonnance* for the handover, bills me for the ride and hurries away. Virginie shows me to my room (yay, it is private, they all are). It has a spacious en suite shower and loo. The shower is 'open plan' in a room clad entirely in marble. The bed is larger. The window is big, my room bright. Everthing is new. The place is spotless.

Good.

*

A bubbly redheaded nurse called Rebecca arrives to draw blood, take my blood pressure and other vital stuff. She slips the hospital bracelet with barcode around my wrist and I feel safe as checked luggage.

Nurse Virginie is back with a dour physician who doesn't introduce himself (his name, I later learn, is Dr Laurence Petitjean). The unsmiling doctor takes a perfunctory look at me. He ascertains that my vision is fucked along with some other stuff but I think he files me under 'not too bad'.

I mention that I had seen a speech therapist in the big hospital and that she had stressed the importance of treatment (she understood my language problems very well; I liked her theoretical and practical dissection of them). Dr Petitjean says he will see what he can do but doesn't. There is no further discussion of this.

*

A nurse's aide comes in to explain the drill at Fignac. We have the choice of dining alone in our rooms or communally in the dining room. This choice is presented in such a way as to steer you away from dining alone like the selfish and miserable fucker you probably are when left to your own devices, and towards the one of almost forcible joining in.

She produces a cloth napkin which we are meant to bring with us to each meal. It will be swapped out for a clean one after breakfast each day.

At the big hospital meals were served about fifteen minutes in advance of the appointed hour. At Fignac they arrive later – not quite on time (and not in a regular way you could learn to set your watch by). This generates a certain unearned, unjustified frisson of anticipation where meals are concerned.

*

Mealtime is also medtime at Fignac (at the big hospital the nurse would deliver your meds about half an hour before meals.

Here the two arrive simultaneously. Which is interesting because the mode of delivery is not confined to oral: some blokes are getting injections, too. At the big hospital injections were accorded the relative privacy of a drawn curtain, but this is not the case at Fignac where they are administered in full view of other patients waiting for their tea.

The nurse stands at the front of the dining room and dispenses from there. We patients stay seated, she brings the stuff (in random order, so far as I can tell).

*

No matter how much I am exposed to it I never tire of French politeness.

Doesn't matter that it is routine, formulaic and scrupulously observed – that is more than half its charm.

I like that when a person enters a room, they greet all the people in that room (*'mesdames, messieurs'*). The social rank of the room's occupants matters not; nor does the nature of the acquaintance (lovers, best friends, colleagues or unknown from Adam): what matters is the duty of politeness.

I have always been a great fan of politeness on the assumption that it is a suppressor of violence (because I think it's harder to fight with a person whom you have just kissed or shaken hands with).

So, here we are, a group of men and women suffering from disabilities as various as recently-amputated limbs to ones that have been palsied or paralyzed by stroke and now we are going to dine together.

*

Men *and* women.

Mixed group.

Coed, as the Americans would say.

My greeting of my fellow diners is also my introduction to them at dinner. (We may have good manners but we are thrown in at the deep end. No one offers their name. Nor does anyone ask mine. The only people who use names are the nurses, who only ever address patients formally.)

*

There are five men and ten women on our ward. The men and women are self-segregated (rather like at school). It reminds me of the automobile spring and foam rubber factory I worked in while a student at the University of Nottingham. There, some of the women would offer sexual favours at lunchtime. Looking around the room I was doubtful if disability would allow it. But, mindful of ageism and prejudice against the disabled I reminded myself, you never know.

I nod and say *'mesdames, messieurs,'* and they say it back at me. I check the vibe of the room and register a major negative from a pair of blokes sat apart from the other men at the rear. Their look sends the hostile alert that has never let me down. I don't know what it is with these dudes. Both are rough-looking (past the obvious signs of working class, they are coarse by choice). One is missing a leg (the bandages tell me it was recently chopped) and the other is also in a wheelchair. They glower menacingly and do not return my greeting.

They are hateful. I have no difficulty imagining tipping them out of their wheelchairs and walking away, leaving them to squirm.

*

The two men sat in front of me are the kind of company I enjoy: polite, quiet, no tendency to excess chatter. The one to my right is missing a leg (also freshly chopped). Like all of the men and most of the women, his background and circumstances are modest. I am struck by his air of determination. He is by no means cheerful. I would say from looking that what he is, is courageous.

Most of these people are a little younger than me. The women all seem younger because they have a certain girlishness about them. I wonder if this is because they are unaccompanied by men. I wonder if they have somehow reverted to an earlier part of their lives (or if this state is always available to them in the absence of men).

When I enter the room, the female greetings are many notches in volume above a mumble. They are curious yet modest. They are delightful. And it's not as if they don't have things to grumble about, 'cos they do. None of them have had any limbs chopped, but all of them use sticks (a few are in wheelchairs).

Unlike the men, they are noisy. And they make a happy noise in spite of their situation. If I shut my eyes I can easily mistake them for a bunch of schoolgirls.

*

The dinner lady brings our trays. (I will get used to the fact that she usually forgets to service my water jug and that I have to ask.) Evening tablets and Kardegic (soluble aspirin) ingested. Now it is time to dig in to evening meal. The expressions on our faces record the verdict upon which we are all agreed.

*

While we are still at table the dinner ladies come around to take our 'orders' for the next day. The only thing wrong with this picture is there is no actual choice (apart from 'special', ie low-sodium and similarly depressing 'options'). But the food, in reality, is not that bad. There are vegetables (tinned) and fruit (fresh) every day. There is beef, veal, fish, chicken, couscous, tripe. Everything is accompanied by a sauce. There is bread. For afters there is fresh fruit or manufactured pudding in a plastic container (in addition to yoghurt or fromage frais). To be honest, it beats the crap out of UK and US hospital fare. The portions are also giant (or my appetite is diminished).

*

I am excited because my brother Brian is coming from the US for a visit tomorrow.

I have only had one visitor since my best mate and old guitar pal from university, Andy Holt, came over from Jersey a couple of weeks ago. (It was no visitors by choice: I wasn't up to it and was in no mood to share my peaceful solitude.)

But my brother is coming all the way from America to see me. In this warm and dusty little corner of Europe.

I am very happy.

*

There is less night noise at Fignac.

That is because there is less activity. After the nurse does her final check for anything you might need, that's it. No one disturbs you until morning.

While it was nice being looked after round-the-clock in the big hospital, it is also nice to experience the greater privacy of Fignac. You felt safe in the big hospital. But the need for that level of safety is over. The care is carefully calibrated. It is portioned out in just the right way.

What a joy it is to be free of IV tubes! You can sleep on your front if you want. You can hug your pillow.

*

On my way to breakfast, Virginie stops me in the corridor. Why am I not wearing my slippers? Actually, her reason for this foot traffic stop is multifarious. It concerns the spoken question but actually implies a number of other things. Firstly, I'm not wearing any slippers because I don't have any slippers? This generates in Virginie's head a number of supplementary questions and judgments: (do I wilfully *refuse* to wear slippers? Can I not afford slippers? Does no one – no woman – care enough about me to provide me with a pair? Do I realize that not wearing slippers can be hazardous?) But, what she really means to say is, *c'est une question de pudeur, monsieur*! 'Pudeur' is an ugly-sounding word for a French emotion that is related to sexual shame, but has an undertone of uncleanliness (for instance, a woman with whom I was visiting Paris was once told off by a chambermaid for accidentally soiling hotel sheets with menstrual blood).

Then she takes me to task for not using my sticks. I explain to her that Dr Gaillard said I no longer needed them, but that I should bring them to Fignac 'just in case'. She fixes me with a look that says 'lying bastard' and makes her way into the dining room to dispense our medication.

*

At breakfast I greet everyone, including the odious men in wheelchairs for whom I have reserved a separate and highly audible *bonjour*.

They glare at me. I adjust my fantasy to include a water feature, so that there is a satisfying splash of their wheelchairs followed by a minute's worth of bubbles.

The dinner lady asks what I would like for breakfast. I know to answer carefully because, if this place is anything like the big hospital, the order will be considered permanent until further notice.

At the big hospital I settled on a breakfast routine that violated all of my pre-Accident rules. I now take apple juice, café au lait with one sugar, four pieces of bread and two servings of butter and preserve (whatever flavour is on offer that day). Pre-Accident I never drank anything other than black coffee at breakfast, never had bread that was untoasted and never had preserve.

While my paralysis is diminishing, I'm still a messy eater. I need to clear the food out of my lap and wash my hands after each meal.

When I get back to my room my bed is made. A cleaner is mopping my bathroom.

*

Yesterday one of the nursing assistants handed me a card on which was written my reeducation schedule. I have three appointments daily, Monday through Friday, weekends off. Hardly a demanding schedule. But I trust the designers of my treatment.

American friends have all stressed the importance of working hard at physiotherapy ('no pain, no gain'). I have been bombarded with advice to 'do what I'm told' and to 'follow orders' – the givers of that advice assuming I will find it physically (and perhaps emotionally) challenging. I actually don't know what to think (why would I know what to think, I've never had a stroke before).

Still, three hours a day seems a light schedule.

Before I came to Fignac I imagined the place as less modern. I imagined what a World War One hospital might have been like and thought of that. I imagined the smell of chlorine from the swimming pool in which locked limbs would be loosened. I imagined a regime of dedicated effort of the sort practiced by the polio-afflicted American president, Franklin D. Roosevelt. The smell of liniment being smoothed on tired muscles. In reality, Fignac is a state of the art reeducation centre dedicated to the treatment of stroke-afflicted persons, paralytics in general, amputees and others suffering from neurological disorders.

*

There is a sign that says *balnéothérapie* (bath treatments) but there is no smell of chlorine and there are no splashing noises.

No odour of menthol from liniment.

I am on the ground floor of the hospital and I am confused. I don't know where to go. I don't know how it can be so confusing, but it is.

Oh, for fuck's sake, there's only two directions. Pick one!

I turn right.

Wrong!

There is a pleasant-looking (but fit and handy) orderly who sees my confusion. We dit bonjour and he asks if he can help. I say I'm looking for the occupational therapy (*ergothérapeute*) department. He leads me there, hands me over to Eric. I think he is just being extra polite. No. He is being extra cautious. He knows, from long experience of stroke patients like me, that we don't know our arses from our elbows. It is safer if no one is lost. If everyone is accounted for.

*

I am busy trying to concentrate on putting impossibly small pegs into equally impossible small holes.

Eric the Viking supervises (if he is going to look this Nordic he's going to be called 'Eric the Viking'). I know that to outsiders my present occupation might seem daft, but the importance of this exercise in developing manual strength and dexterity is clear to me from the outset. What is more, all of these occupational therapy exercises are very cleverly designed to show measurable daily progress and satisfy a deeply-rooted need for success. I bang my fists together in childlike delight (if I could clap, I would).

*

Noon. There is a tentative knock at the door and then my brother appears. We hug.

I can see his surprise (or is it envy?) at my weight loss.

Since I have stopped shaving I don't much notice myself in the mirror.

As always we achieve an instant comfort level, but I can sense his curiosity about how serious was my stroke. I tell him (but I can see from his reaction that I am still underestimating). I think he can imagine the progress I've made. He also understands better than I do how far off I am from recovery. He can see how fucked I am. I've grown used to it.

He has just come from the airport. We spend a happy hour together before my physiotherapy appointment.

*

Knock me down with a feather.

Or push me very, very gently with the tips of your fingers. 'Cos that's all it takes.

Today I am having my first physiotherapy session with Tomas. We are working on balance.

This is not about learning ballet. It is practical stuff about not falling over. And it is very, very difficult.

I have never been one for balance. (Ask anyone: my views, my sense of *equilibre*, as the French call it, have never been anywhere close to perfect.) Post-The Accident, I have virtually none. Where has it gone?

I guess I have lost it.

I know that if there were any normal people here to look at me, the first thing they would notice is, *hey, look at that bloke, he's lost his sense of balance!*

Luckily there are no normal people here.

*

Yanis is standing in the first floor corridor with a stopwatch in his hand.

Yanis is in charge of exercise at Fignac, and he reminds me of my high school track coach, Mr Scott. The only difference is that when Mr Scott held the stopwatch I was a young athlete. Now, I am a disabled person who is almost qualified for his bus pass.

But the anticipatory buzz, as I toe the starting line, is nearly identical. This is my chance to establish a personal best in the men's 1 km hallway post-Accident walk.

Go!

I wonder what pace I should set for myself. I don't want to run out of steam before the finish. Yanis helps me keep track of distance by calling out each fifty metres I have covered. Halfway through I realize I have enough puff to increase my pace considerably. (I stubbed out what I hope will be my last cigarette as I entered the hospital. The percentage of hospital workers who smoke is quite high).

I can't remember my time that afternoon, but I was quite pleased by it.

And I know I can do better.

*

As I make my way to breakfast I find myself face-to-belt-buckle with one of the two scowling wheelchair blokes. He sees it is inevitable our paths will cross and looks up. Doesn't smile, but nods his head curtly in what passes for a *bonjour*. He takes his place next to his scowling friend and resumes his usual attitude.

I say hello to the ladies and good morning to my male colleagues. It strikes me how different they all are, these people, my fellow patients. There are fine gradations of class. The women seem, on the whole, fitter than the men.

One of the women is more animated than the rest. She is the youngest among us by at least ten years. Her speech, her accent, exaggerates perfect pronunciation. At first I find her mannered, affected. Slightly annoying. By the end of breakfast her volubility, her enthusiasm, have made me laugh. She has entertained me. In fact, she has charmed me.

The man I am sat next to is, I would guess, a professional. An engineer? I might have guessed medical, but I imagine that doctors might opt for private care (I don't know if this is true or not, the public care is so good.) He smiles when I sit down. He is very likable. Whatever visible disability he might have suffered from appears to be dissipating.

*

I have been wondering when Eric the PT is going to give me a rubber ball to squeeze.

Not today.

He does, however, give me a hand grip with a complex web of elastic bands for tension. The device has a sinister, specialist cripple equipment look (and feel) to it. I get my hand round it and squeeze. The result is disappointing (actually, it is negligible). Eric adjusts the thing to make it a bit (but only a bit) easier. Okay, here is a starting point. (I imagine the instruction manual for this device indicates that the present setting is 'cream puff').

We proceed with more grippy stuff. Pinching, actually. Miniature, brightly-coloured clothes pegs.

A milestone on the road to recovery from a paralyzed hand is to be able to touch each of your fingertips to your thumb. I can (sort of) do this, but not with ease, never mind panache.

But I am getting there.

Then scissors, to cut out fractal shapes from stiffish, thin cardboard. I am immediately confronted by angles (obtuse and acute). My scissors are poised over the problem. Rather than cutting around the shape (which will surely give a messy result) I cut a straight line and then another which joins it, and watch the pieces fall away. I look to Eric for approval (for an answer to my implied question, *is this allowed*?). He smiles and nods.

I'm a good boy.

*

My brother is going to shave me.

He offered.

Emmanuelle did it a few times at the big hospital. I had never been shaved before that.

It's an odd feeling, being shaved. Slightly nervous-making. I suppose it's got to do with trust (razors, throats, etc.)

The first time I touched a black person was when I worked as a janitor in the county old folks home. I was seventeen in my hometown in upstate New York. His name was Fred. He was a wizened old man and I liked him enormously. The fact that this poor man washed up in our whiter-than-white, small town, bigoted environment is proof (if you ever needed it) that there is no god and, if there were, it is anything but merciful. Fred was shunned by everyone. They treated him as if he smelt bad. In truth, he stank of piss, like the majority of residents. Fred wanted a haircut and no one would do it. (Frightened they might catch cooties, I expect.) He had a set of hair clippers in his luggage. I shaved his head.

I caught hell for it from the nurse.

Fred died a few days later.

*

Brian taps at the door. I answer and he holds up bags containing razor blades and shaving gel.

Yay.

And one containing a beard trimmer thingy. With a silly number of attachments. Even my brother, who subscribes to the 'more is better' school of choice, is spoiled mute.

We separate and isolate most of the equipment as surplus to requirements.

My brother and I stand looking at ourselves in the big bathroom mirror. 'I think you should sit,' he says.

'Okay.'

He fits the beard trimming attachment and the thing buzzes into life. He presses it to my chin and

I can feel the temperature change as the thick hair is trimmed from my face.

'Take your shirt off,' my brother suggests.

He finishes the first trim of facial hair, switches off the machine and blows on it to remove the clogged hair. He slips the attachment off to reveal the blade. 'I'll just shave closer to your skin.' He does, and it tickles a little bit.

'Okay, I think it's time to lather up,' my brother says.

I agree. He shakes the can of shaving gel and squirts some into his hand. Rubs his hands together to activate the mousse and spreads it carefully on my face. Wipes his hands in preparation for shaving.

Begins to shave me.

You can hear how sharp are the blades as they cut through my beard. My brother rinses the razor under the gently running tap and resumes.

I like the way you can keep track of where you are with shaving. It's satisfying, like shovelling snow.

He uses a towel to wipe my face clean.

'There! All done!' he exclaims. 'Want me to trim your nose hair?'

I do.

It tickles.

*

My brother has already had his lunch and makes room for the nursing assistant to bring mine.

(I announced earlier to Virginie that I would be dining in my room because my brother was coming, but I am not sure if she thought this an adequate excuse for what is clearly considered an antisocial act).

The scent of shaving gel lingers on my face. Normally I shower after I have shaved, but today is different.

My brother waits for the nursing assistant to leave. He nods at my lunch. 'Any good?'

I survey my lunch. Couscous with vegetables and lamb. Slice of bread. Applesauce. Fromage frais. Not bad.

'No bad,' I say.

'Good,' he replies.

It is odd that however much I look forward to something (like a visit from my brother), the tiniest taste of it satisfies. To the extent that I can say, 'okay, did that.'

Which is not to say that I am bored with my brother's visit, and won't feel sadness when it is over. I know my brother feels this, too.

I would feel this same odd emotion when visiting my mother when I travelled from London.

Bags of anticipation. Then, after a couple of hours, I'd be phoning my mates to see if they wanted to go to the pub.

I finish my lunch.

My brother stands. 'I've got a lot of work this afternoon. I'll see you tomorrow.'

We shake hands.

'See you tomorrow, bro.'

*

Whatever I may have said about French physiotherapy vis-à-vis stroke recovery not being strenuous, I take it back.

Strenuous. Fuck strenuous. It's torture.

*

Tomas is doing an excellent job of physiotorture on me today.

I have noticed, in the weeks since The Accident, an odd and rare absence of physical pain. No chronic sciatic pain. No headaches, backaches, neck aches, muscle aches: an absence of aches. And pains.

Tomas has reintroduced me. Yesterday's apparently gentle session turns out to have been anything but. And now I can add to the extreme pain of my balance exercises a thrilling new element: fear. Total fear of falling. I know Tomas says he will catch me, but I am not confident that he can. ('You're tall, Monsieur Trombley'. *I know; I'm heavy, too!*)

I had to be confident in my brother's ability not accidentally to slit my throat while shaving it and he's not even a professional barber. Christ, Tomas does physiotherapy for a living, you'd think I might cut him a little slack.

*

Near enough silent, extremely deadly.

At least the potential to be deadly.

Yanis's blowgun, but sans the poison darts.

A key weapon in the stroke recovery arsenal is the blowgun. It might seem at first an odd tool, but it is genius.

You use it while standing on a thick, squidgy foam mat that challenges your balance. The blowgun is about four feet long and uses a dart that is about four and a half inches. It provides a wide range of exercises and progress indicators.

Stroke can impair respiration and this exercise (with its demand for a deep breath) helps. We also tend to get dizzy after the exertion of breathing deeply and blowing hard; this helps with that. After a stroke a very common visual disturbance is the problem of skewed vision (it is difficult to blow a dart accurately). Achieving a straight line is very difficult especially when you are wobbling and are running out of puff. Just loading the thing is a very useful exercise in itself as it teaches manual dexterity and hand-to-eye coordination at distances not routinely tested.

These physical exercises are brilliantly conceived and mimic real-world situations (driving, for instance: turning your head, focusing, aiming the car in a straight line, performing multiple tasks simultaneously).

The blowgun is a bastard to use. Early on I counted just hitting the non-score edge of the target as a major victory.

It is bags of infuriating fun. And it is easy to measure progress with it. You begin by missing the target altogether as you search for your range. By the end of day one you discover the amount of force required to hit the target. Actually achieving a score will take a little longer.

*

Vending machines are among the great allures of public spaces in hotels and hospitals.

Cookies. Pretzels. Nuts. Candy.

You name it, they got it. (Even things you didn't even know you needed, until they suggested it).

There I was, on my back in the big hospital hospital for five weeks, with no access to snacks. Now I am at Fignac, with its twenty-four access to packaged treats.

For me!

And anyone else with a pocketful of change.

My first trip to the vending machine is a failure inasmuch as I forget to bring money.

I haven't handled any for five weeks.

I go back upstairs. (I elect to use the stairs rather than take the lift; it is a challenging physical workout and safety exercise/balance test).

When I come back down I reach into my pocket for my change. I have placed it in a plastic bag. Which is handy, 'cos that stops it from rolling all over the place when I drop it like I just did. (My movements are tentative, slow and slow and ponderous. I look around to see if I have inconvenienced anyone who might be queueing behind me – I haven't.). I pick up my money. I am clutching it awkwardly, as if with a claw. I carefully use both hands to free some change from the bag. Then I drop it again and it goes everywhere.

I bend over and begin to pick it up. I want to shout at the lady who has crouched down alongside me to help (don't want her help, want to get used to cleaning up my own mess). But I don't shout at her. Instead, I thank her before getting up. I let her go ahead of me (*no, really, I insist*). As she walks away I spill my change for the third time.

After I finish picking it up I walk over to a nearby table and dump it there. I go back to the machine to check the price of a bag of peanuts. I knew it a moment ago, but I have forgotten again. It involves three coins (unless I shove a two euro coin in.) But then there will be change. There is no way of predicting *how much* change. (The value of the currency, yes; but the amount of change, the number of coins, no.) I elect to insert the right money.

Separating and getting control of three coins of different sizes is difficult. Holding them up to the machine and inserting them is even more so.

Eventually I am successful. I put the rest of the change back in my pocket and climb the stairs.

That wasn't so bad. Could've been worse.

Fucking took long enough.

*

Shock Corridor....

And countless other 1950s black and white movies depicting life in the loony bin.

That's what the male nurses and physiotherapy orderlies at Fignac remind me of: orderlies in an insane asylum.

Unfair to orderlies, I am certain. (I just find fit blokes dressed in white uniforms while wearing crepe-soled shoes and pushing wheelchairs creepy.)

The bloke who supervises putting us to bed has crepe soles. His short sleeves and bare arms suggest nudity. Unfair to him I'm sure, but it creeps me out anyway.

There is a lot of wishing good night with this nurse.

Good night, I say decisively.

And then he asks have I done caca today….

*

'Let's go on a day trip,' I suggest to my brother.

He looks up from his computer. 'Where?'

'Restaurant. Lunch.'

'Think they'll let us?'

'We can ask.'

'Cool. Make it happen.'

*

Eric has a big surprise for me today.

We are going to do writing.

We have already done tying our shoes, picking up a cigarette lighter (!) and pouring a kettle of (cold) water.

Now, for the first time since The Accident, I am holding a pen in my right hand; in what used to be my good but which is now my fucked hand.

Eric has set in front of me a child's handwriting exercise sheet featuring the letter 'A'.

I remember the last time I tried to write. I was having a stroke. The handwriting (it feels too odd to call it 'my handwriting') was illegible. But that wasn't the scary thing about it. *It was tiny as well as illegible!*

It was unrecognizable as mine.

I had written, *je suis en détresse* ('I am in distress').

It was downright sinister.

Never mind the content of the message: the handwriting itself told you all you needed to know. This was an emergency. A medical emergency. A big medical emergency.

A cerebrovascular accident.

*

The trouble with Eric's alphabet is that is in French!

No, really. You know how Europeans make funny-looking sevens and add all sorts of curly stuff to their writing? That. But with knobs on.

I am doing my best trying to copy Eric's foreign alphabet. But, I have just had a stroke and I am not doing so good.

'Do I have to draw it just like this?' I ask.

'Yes,' says Eric.

Okay, I will keep trying.

But I don't see the point. I never l learned to write like this in the first place, so why try to 'relearn' what I never knew? Also, I just have terrible handwriting. Maybe it's because the nuns beat me on my hands, across my knuckles, for the same reason: I couldn't do cursive.

So I taught myself to make block capitals.

*

I score a day pass from the nurse!

She had to ask the doctor. She made clear that I might have left it too late, as it was a Friday.

I didn't mention that the idea of freedom only occurred to me yesterday.

I tell my brother the news. 'Good,' he says.

*

Late afternoon coffee.

Who ever heard of such a thing?

At four-thirty p.m. a nursing assistant knocks at the door offering it.

With a biscuit!

Yes, please.

Every afternoon. Four-thirty. Monday through Friday. Expresso.

Whether you were planning to sleep or not.

*

I am very nervous.

It's the day pass.

It's one thing to practise walking in the safety of hospital and another altogether to be 'free' for a whole afternoon – free to go to a café, and then to a restaurant – free to wobble horribly on the concrete steps, free to fall with a sickening thud, followed by sharp pain.

But there is no pain, no thud. Because I do not fall. I just wobble. Badly, but I catch myself. This is one of those situations in which 'almost' doesn't even come close to counting.

There was careful safety checking before I was temporarily released from hospital.

Is this your brother?

Yes.

Where are you going?

Lunch.

Where?

La Vielle Auberge. (Nurse raises eyebrows).

What time will you return?

Four p.m.

A tout à l'heure

Yeah, we're going to La Vielle Auberge, but first we're stopping at the boozer (oops, I mean café): Le Campus.

*

My brother drives the car. I marvel at his ability to do it.

I know that it is beyond me.

We pull into a parking space in front of Le Campus. *Bless me, father, it is five weeks since I've taken a drink....*

We sit outside. It's a sunny day, trying to be warm. My brother and I are both having a half of lager.

'Just one,' my brother cautions.

'Okay.'

I tell my brother that I had stumbled across this boozer while buying cigarettes at the tabac opposite. It looked a dreary, characterless place at first. Now it was one of my two locals.

'Maybe just one more half,' I say.

'Okay. But just one more.'

'Okay.'

'So, most of the furniture in my house comes from a *brocante* less than two miles up the road,' I say.

My brother remarks that it is nice furniture (most of it dates from the 1930s).

'It was cheap,' I add.

'Good,' he replies.

'I'll have a pastis with ice.' I explain what pastis is. My brother brings it.

'They delivered it for free.'

'What did they deliver for free?'

'The furniture.'

'Oh yeah. The furniture.'

My brother and I agree that we have consumed an ample sufficiency of apéritifs. He helps me to the car and we drive the five hundred metres to the restaurant.

*

'Bonjour, chef!'

The owner of La Vielle Auberge greets me with a big smile and even bigger handshake. He notices my palsied arm right away. Lessens his grip but does not let go of my hand.

I explain where I've been, partly by way of apology for my absence (La Vielle Auberge is my regular luncheon venue). He pooh-poohs that, says he just wants to see me better. His wife comes over and greets me. I reintroduce them (and their dog) to Brian (the dog has not forgotten that Brian was here at Christmas). We are shown to our table.

Brian opens his menu. 'What are we going to have?'

'Foie gras, glass of Monbazzilac. Plat du jour. *Café gourmand.*' (I explain that this is espresso accompanied by a selection of small dessert items).

'Okay, but what about the wine?'

'Half bottle of Chinon, Loire Valley red you drink chilled, can go fish or meat.'

'Done.'

My brother chooses gibelotte de lapin aux cèpes (a kind of rabbit stew with wild mushrooms) as his main course. I opt for filet steak with Périgueux (Madeira and truffle) sauce.

It is a marvellous meal. Wonderful company, generous and talented hosts, delicious food and wine.

Until it begins to go pear-shaped.

It is difficult to pinpoint the onset of post-stroke-I-don't-feel-so-good and to describe the phenomenon accurately (its pervasiveness interferes with its localization). The symptoms are, I don't feel so good, aggravated by extreme tiredness.

My brother, a seasoned drinker like myself, inquires, 'do you think you've had too much to drink?'

I reply, much to my surprise, 'yes.' (Hospital has taught me two things: there is no sense in not being truthful; and that what might have been true six weeks ago isn't necessarily true now (for instance, that three aperitifs, a glass of Monbazillac and a glass and a half of Chinon are enough to make me pissed).

My dinner was terrific (as expected). My brother's, on the other hand, was fucking delicious. It really was.

The only possible complaint is that we scrimped on the wine (but see above).

Halfway through my *café gourmand* I take a funny turn.

I am suddenly very tired. Deeply fatigued.

'The bill,' I say to my brother.

He doesn't blink. Gets up immediately to fetch it.

I go outside and steady myself. I hold on to the restaurant. The owner brings a chair.

My brother appears, we make our way to the car.

My brother helps me into the lift and to my room. Luckily there are no nurses to witness our return. He makes sure my shoes are off and I am sitting on the bed before he leaves.

'That was a great lunch,' my brother says.

I agree. 'It was fabulous.'

*

The letter, 'B'.

Upper case.

It's got more curlicues than a Spanish wrought iron door.

Eric and I did this on Friday, except it was with an 'A': we attempted joined-up writing. But I made a mess of it. The American (I was taught by American nuns, Sisters of 'Mercy') alphabet looks nothing like the French one.

'Do your best,' Eric instructs.

I grumble.

This is nearly impossible. I am clutching the pen in my palsied hand. It is hard to keep it straight, to keep the ink end of it pointed at the page. These French shapes of the letters of the alphabet are strange to me. I am drawing them for the first time.

Eric looks at my work. Assesses my skill at copying the alphabet. And there it is, what I've been waiting for from him: the slightest hint of a frown!

*

Yanis introduces me to Tina in the gym.

I've watched her in here before. She is small, blonde, has a tidy figure. There is a hint of mischief about her.

'We are going to play a game today,' she says.

'Really?' I ask.

'Yes,' she says, in a tone that indicates work has begun. Tina explains that she is going to take me on a tour of the hospital. Every time we change direction, she will mark the spot with a little numbered sign.

Ah. We are embarking on an orienteering exercise. What fun!

Actually, a mild panic comes over me. Every day that I am here, the same thing happens: I take wrong turns in the corridors. Even with repetition and a fifty-fifty chance of getting it right, I get it wrong.

Tina smiles at me, takes the lead. I like looking at her moving in front of me. She looks back to make sure I am following, slows her pace a little to let me catch up.

'Number One,' she announces, setting the marker opposite the lift where it arrives at the first floor. She makes sure I have clocked the location, then presses on. We go down a corridor that is unfamiliar to me and Tina deposits marker Number Two on a table. And so on. (I was lost shortly after marker Number One).

Tina deposits the last marker and leads me back to the beginning.

'Okay, show me,' she challenges.

I get the first one, no trouble. And the second. I hesitate on the direction for Number Three. But wait. Did Tina just indicate, with an almost imperceptible nod of her head, the direction I should follow?

I go there and, guess what?

I think Tina must be a good memory teacher. She delivers me back to Yanis and reports, 'perfect score.' She gives me a smile and walks away.

Yanis makes a mark on his clipboard and says we are done for today.

*

Alain, the bloke who sits next to me in the dining room who had his leg chopped, is having a new artificial one fitted today.

The unveiling of it is an unheralded event. But, as the hour for its maiden walk in the physiotherapy room approaches, the behaviour of the women begins to acquire a furtive quality. The attendant wheels Alain to the waiting room which has a long corridor that patients use for walking. The other patients pretend they aren't looking.

Alain's new leg doesn't look like anything special, but I know that it is an incredibly complex machine.

Alan prepares to push himself up out of his wheelchair.

The room goes quiet.

He stands in front of the Zimmer frame the orderly has placed there.

He takes one step.

Then a second.

Then a third.

The patients resume their conversations.

I am sat in the waiting room, a couple of metres in front of Alain. It occurs to me that, had we been in the United States, a great cheer for Alain would have been raised (which the French might have judged sentimental and a little vulgar).

*

I am walking (well, wobbling) in a straight line with my eyes shut.

It is a physiotherapy balance exercise. Tomas is walking alongside me. I feel like telling him I don't need someone to spot me when there's no danger of falling. We're on a flat surface, for Christ's sake.

Tomas tells me to stop and to open my eyes.

Holy cow!

I can't believe it!

I've veered a whole lot of degrees away from a straight line. A lot.

The other patients laugh at me.

They laugh because what I just did is laughable.

I join in their laughter until tears run down my face.

It is good, this laughter. It is cleansing. It is a laughter shared among equals. Among men and women 'of a certain age' who are physically and mentally fucked. There is mutual recognition of shared identity and otherness, etc, etc.

But, basically, it is just plain funny.

You, the reader, however, are forbidden to laugh. You would be guilty of ableism.

The physiotherapists are not allowed to laugh, either.

They would be guilty of mocking the afflicted.

Only the afflicted can mock the afflicted.

*

Competition and ridicule.

Triumph, embarrassment.

Tenderness. Compassion.

Fignac can be a tough environment. It is not necessarily a place where the overly sensitive will be comfortable.

It is a place of adult emotions.

I think that if you want insight into a nation's culture, you can do worse than to observe its response to emergencies and its care for the sick. There are national styles of compassion, care, humour.

I like the French approach to this stuff.

*

Tomas will occasionally break into English when instructing me.

Execrable, poorly pronounced, ungrammatical, English. I find this tendency annoying, and one day I exclaim (too loudly, I recognize too late), *'Parler en francais, s'il vous plaît! Mon français est meilleur que votre anglais!'* ('Speak French, please! My French is better than your English!').

It was rude, but the other physiotherapists in the room (all women) laugh.

Tomas eventually laughs, too.

They laugh because I made a fair comment. My remark is true. Truth trumps politeness and so is exempt from its rules (which only apply if my statement had been false).

'Il est portugais,' ('He's Portuguese') says one of the physios, laughing. As it by way of apology.

I feel a little bad. English is the bloke's third (or fourth) language for fuck's sake. Most Americans can only speak one language (and not very well).

A week later Tomas has got me playing video balance games (skiing, trying not to bump into people while walking, etc). He asks me if I like Charles Bukowski. I stop what I'm doing and look at him.

'Yes, I do.'

Tomas nods seriously, as if to say, *'I thought you might'*.

We talk a little about Bukowski's poetry and his novel *Ham on Rye*, which Tomas enjoyed.

Then he quizzes me about my bibliography.

*

'Want to try the expert setting?'

Louise is standing in for Tomas, who has taken a week's holiday (it is the Feast of the Ascension). She is a plain, monotasking girl who keeps me waiting forty-five minutes at our first session.

She adjusts the computer game to its new setting. The revision has me on my toes. I speed up and lean into the turn. I experience the same disappointment I did the first time I played this game. Then, the gates seemed to fly by and, no matter how much I anticipated them, they were gone long before I could execute my turn. The fact of being late for the last gate guaranteed I would miss the next one and I soon learned intentionally to skip one in order to prepare for the next. (I know this is against the rules in real ski racing, but these ain't real skis).

But this time I know that what seemed an impossible task isn't. So I chill. Which helps my performance no end. By my third go, I am getting all the gates on the expert setting (not at top speed, mind).

As for the other game, the one where you have to avoid pedestrians: I've left a load of them bruised and prostrate in my wake.

*

Soul clapping.

If you don't know what I'm talking about, please turn the page now.

Soul clapping is the infectious R&B rhythm made famous by Archie Bell and the Drells with their 1968 hit record 'Tighten Up'. Its effect is to fox white people.

I suppose that making music is still my second favourite thing to do. When I was sixteen I got a guitar and I've spent chunks of my life my life making songs on it. When asked (by hospital admission staff, for instance), 'what is your profession?', I tell them, 'writer.' I think that covers all the bases.

I am sitting at Eric's work table, waiting for him to finish a report before the start of our occupational therapy session. I am trying to clap my hands. (I don't know why. This activity is instinctive. I just find myself doing it from time to time).

After The Accident I couldn't do it. First of all, I lacked the coordination to do it. Secondly, I lacked the strength. And, thirdly, my hand was paralyzed.

After a few weeks I could do a really limp-wristed version of clapping. Actually, it wasn't so much clapping as striking my right hand with my left one.

For some reason, the activity of clapping is important to me, but I had never paid it much (conscious) attention. Clapping as in applause? Or as tuneless musical accompaniment?

Who knows.

Then, one day, I am sitting in Eric's office and I start soul clapping. Just like that. From nowhere.

I am overjoyed. Excited, I show Eric.

I watch him look at me, patiently. (I'm sure they have a manual in which it says, *never discourage them.*)

Yeah, baby. I just soul clapped. (It is still my most memorable recovery moment).

*

I wonder if it is like sex torture.

My eyes are shut. It's not like I don't have a choice. I am not wearing a blindfold. But I keep my eyes shut anyway, 'cos it would be cheating to peek.

And then there is the pain. Screaming, intense pain.

In my thighs.

I guess it is my willingness to go along with physical therapy, my consent, that gives it a sexual tone.

It is awful. It is agony.

But it is suffering brought on by desire.

Desire to get better.

All submission to medical procedures that make you better contains a sexual element. There is consent (surrender). Force is also applied. And there is sexual content in that: both in the passivity and in the endurance through gritted teeth.

*

The fact of paralysis is mentally testing.

The most obvious thing about it is that you can't see it. There is nothing *to* see. It's invisible!

Then *how*, you might ask, *can something that is invisible weigh so much*?

How much does a paralyzed limb weigh? Try lifting one: a hundred pounds at least, right? Maybe more.

Paralyzed limbs are infuriating. No matter how hard you push them – or pull them – they will not budge. They are immovable.

They are heavy. That is all.

If you try to move a paralyzed limb you will break into a sweat. And then you will experience an associated taste: tears.

Why would you cry? Frustration is one reason. But, to be honest, that is small beer. The big one, the main reason you might cry is the realization that you may well have used that limb for the last time (at full capacity, anyway).

It might be time to start mourning the loss of the use of your limb.

*

I am lying on my back, staring at the ceiling, idly playing with myself (as blokes do when no one is watching).

We've had our tea. The telly is on, but I am not watching it.

Le Carré's *The Looking Glass War* lies unopened on my bed (waiting for me to be ready; if I manage it this will be my fourth time).

The nurse, Mélissa, comes in. I don't move my hands off my genitals. (Why the fuck should I? This is a private room and she is in it.)

As luck would have it, Mélissa is not plain. At all. In fact, she is hands down the most attractive nurse on the ward.

I admire the way she totally ignores me having half a wank. She asks if I need anything. I say, 'no'. She asks if I have made *caca*. I say, 'yes'. She smiles and says good night.

*

I had seen old people walking with ski poles.

In America.

They looked daft.

(What is wrong with this picture? *There isn't any snow*, you pillock.)

Yanis is rooting around in the toy cupboard. He produces three pairs of non-snow ski poles. Nordic ski poles (for that is the name of this game).

The third pair is for Jeanne, who is new. She is the youngest of our group (mid-forties?) and she is late for our session.

Yanis does not tell us how to do it.

I watch Yanis. I copy him.

I wonder about the breathing. How/where should breaths occur?

Naturally. That's where they should occur, I decide.

This is the French way: *just do it*.

Yanis is in the lead.

Jeanne lags behind. When I turn to look at her she rolls her eyes as if to say, *fuck this for a game of soldiers*.

There is something very likable about Jeanne. She's got spirit.

Yanis slows and waits for us to catch up.

*

Since my hospital experience in France has provided me with ample opportunity to sniff a range of their armpits, I want to talk about 'the French' and personal hygiene.

A significant proportion of Americans think the French are 'dirty' (the English, too, but they don't count 'cos they just hate the French generally). Why do 'foreigners' think that?

So I Googled it and came across this thread: 'Why are the French sometimes regarded as dirty people?'* To kick things off, Séverine Godet (a French expat) who is a marketing consultant writes:

> I wonder if for the US People it is linked to the fact that when GI's discovered France during WWII they arrived in a country (and through the country side of Normandy) that

was economically not as developed as the US. At that time having toilets inside your home wasn't the norm (It was often in the garden backhouse), People did not all have running water / bathrooms (they cleaned in a cold bucket). Even in Paris the hygienic situation was decades behind the US one, and don't forget it was the war with all its restrictions on supplies! Many US people remember this France, and told tales about it to their families, while there is a huge 70 years gap between this memory and the present day and norms in France.

That seems like a reasonable explanation. But what about the English?

Another explanation for the Brits...is that they had regular encounters with French fishermen/fishmongers and onion sellers that had to cross the Channel on boat/bike to bring delicacies to the markets, so they sure reeked of... Fish and onion! :)

Séverine then invites the forum to 'tell me your thoughts about that, time to come clean in this topic. :)' 'Anonymous' writes, 'I'd say some French people have a horrible hygiene. They don't bathe or take showers everyday. Worse, they usually use a washcloth to clean their face, armpits AND genitals at the same time when they're too lazy showering before going to work/school in the morning or, another excuse, when it's too cold in the winter.'

Crikey.

'Anonymous' concludes, 'I first thought it was a countryside thing, but when I moved to Paris, same here. That's why we have such bad body odour in the Paris subway in the morning.'

We.

Ian Raskin, a 'history buff', who has 'spent about half my life outside America, but American', says 'I read a US army pamphlet on the topic as some advice to US troops to remember that during the occupation everything – including soap and hot water had been in short supply during the occupation.' A nice observation that offers an 'explanation' of French hygiene without apologizing for it.

Isabelle Salshe writes that 'Old anglo-saxon myth, rivalries throughout history etc etc..denigrate your enemy.' She adds, 'Strange because I have never entered a French household which was less than spotless (although am sure there are dirty homes)'.

And, finally, Jon Reed. A librarian from New York City who writes: 'I lived in different countries, including France.' Jon has three complaints about French hygiene. He says that 'In Paris the Parisians won't cover their mouths when they cough or sneeze. That is very unhygienic.' He also observes that 'Men (regular businessmen, not homeless ones) will pee on the sides of streets (main roads, not alleys) in broad daylight.' But I think his chief complaint is that 'Dental floss is not commonly found (I would buy it at first sight if I encountered it, no matter what I was in the store buying originally, and no matter the cost of the floss.)' Jon explains that these things 'were all experienced personally by me, frequently.'

Jon addresses the 'body odour' issue. 'The next thing I heard countless expats say was that the French in France smell from bad body odor. I personally didn't notice any body odor proportionately worse than in the US.' But Jon saves his last jaw-dropping complaint for his conclusion: 'In Paris I heard many stories from expat women and some French women, about men behaving like perverts, such as openly masturbating while staring at them from 15 feet away at Parc Monceau or following them through Paris first flirting but after being rebuffed, saying lewd sexual stuff and still following them.'

Blimey.

I think that Séverine's remarks about World War Two and memory (there are only half a million surviving US veterans from World War Two and not all of those served in France) are true and go a long way to explain the perpetuation of the idea of French 'uncleanliness'. I think we can all agree that the French are famous for their fine cuisine; if we happen to be English we can try as hard as we like to counter this inconvenient truth with the slander of 'filthy French muck' served by 'filthy French bastards'. Similarly, the American obsession with 'clean' odours is trumped by Coco Chanel, Christian Dior and others (though it is understood that what Americans often mean by cleanliness has more to do with asepsis than it does with smelling good).

The French don't taste of soap.

*

Crack.

Poof.

Thud.

Odd noises.

Sounds like gunshots.

But it's springtime. It's not hunting season.

'Maybe it's to scare the crows,' my brother suggested. We had seen a few scarecrows in the fields.

Jeanne and I are chugging along behind Yanis with our Nordic ski poles. We are huffing and puffing our way along roads whose fields are planted with wheat and with grapes for Pineau de Charentes.* (As the seasons progress the fields will give way to rapeseed, sunflowers, corn, hay.) The hospital is surrounded by farms. In fact, it it might be more accurate to describe the scene as farms with a hospital among them rather than as a hospital surrounded by farms.

Yanis keeps a close eye on us while we cross the road. It is a warm and sunny day. I notice that Jeanne is a little short of breath. I have her pegged as an ex-smoker who is struggling with it.

The day after The Accident Dr Gaillard asked if I needed any assistance quitting smoking. I told him I didn't think I did. I mean, I just nearly fucking died of it, right?

In the big hospital I was on the wards and so not subject to cigarette smoke. The second I exited the hospital I could smell it. Nurses were doing it. I ignored it. I thought, *no*.

Fignac, with its lack of restrictions in all areas, meant smoking was no longer prohibited.

But I did not want to smoke. Why would I?

I looked at the smokers loitering outside the entrance. Actually found myself staring at them. (It's late August right now, and have been craving a snout since early July. Haven't had one, though.)

We make the final turn and head for home.

'Yanis?' I ask.

He looks at me and widens his eyes to indicate I have his attention.

'Hear that sound'? (The shot-like noise has just happened again.)

'Yes,' says Yanis. 'Epouvantail' ('scarecrow').

*

I am confronted with the problem of how to eat a pear when my neighbour Alain unfolds his pocket knife and hands it to me.

The scene transports me forty years into the past, watching a man whom I guessed to be Algerian squatting while cutting and eating fruit with a knife.

It was in front of Orange railway station in Provence. He was sitting on his heels. I remember being impressed by the keenness of the blade's edge because of the ease with which it sliced through the flesh. (I remember noticing that not much juice was lost because of this.)

I was in Orange hitchhiking with my brother and the girlfriend of a friend. We were looking for work during the *vendange* (grape harvest). We had stopped at a café near the station to enquire. The owner shrugged in that Gallic way that not only indicates 'I don't know', but also, *I don't like you* and, *why don't you fuck off.*

The entire café looks at us like we are out of our minds. We start walking along a D road, hitchhiking. It is not very long before a car stops. A blonde woman in her forties invites us to lunch; says she knows a few growers and will make calls. We arrive at a posh, modern house with a lovely garden.

She introduces her husband who is a doctor. I have just started work on my PhD (Virginia Woolf and her doctors) and he and I have a lively conversation that lasts all afternoon. Meanwhile Madam has prepared a wonderful lunch which features the best tomato salad I have ever tasted. When we leave, we have a job picking grapes at Domaine Pierre Quoiot (Châteauneuf-du-Pape). Our hostess has lent us three bicycles and dropped us at a campsite convenient for the château where we will work.

It is hard to believe our luck. We started our journey without work in Beeston (Nottinghamshire) that morning and ended in the South of France with jobs by the end of the afternoon.

The task involves clipping bunches of grapes from the vines and laying them in big, rectangular plastic tubs. The overseer (slave driver) is a stout, red faced fellow. He is gruff, but I like him. There are frequent water breaks. Most of the workers are Algerian migrants. Part of my work assignment is to carry the full tubs of grapes to a farm wagon, then return the tub when it is empty. As I walk past the Algerian men, they laugh and cry out, *burro, burro*.

Day one is hot and backbreaking. So hot and so backbreaking that my brother quits at the end of it. My friend's girlfriend leaves the next day.

That leaves just me to enjoy the remainder of the fortnight's pre-term break. I love it. The work is hard, but I am young and strong. Towards the end of my stay, the cloth-capped men in the café begin to acknowledge my presence.

I make friends with a lovely old man and his granddaughter (who is starting university when we finish the harvest). He gives me a lift to the vineyard every morning in his old Renault 4, memorable because its gearbox is mounted flat against the dashboard. The three of us lunch together every day, watching the Algerian women serve steaming bowls of couscous to their men while we eat our baguette and Brie.

When my stint at Domaine Pierre Quiot is over, M Quiot pays me in cash and gives me two bottles of wine. I call the doctor's wife to return the bicycles and set off on my hitchhike home. I catch a left almost immediately from the manager of jazz violinist Jean-Luc Ponty, of whose music I am a fan. He takes me all the way from Orange to a wonderful restaurant in the Paris suburbs (he has a quiet word with the maitre'd who excuses my extremely casual attire). I have langoustines, blanquette de veau and chocolate mousse. It is the finest meal I have ever eaten (at this point).

At the end of the evening he drives me to an inexpensive hotel and I arrive in Nottingham a couple of days later.

I wipe Alain's pen knife, fold it and hand it back to him with thanks.

*

Vous parlez bien francais, monsieur Trombley!

Nice of you to say, but I don't really think so.

Mais oui, c'est parfait.

My French is anything but perfect, but it is nice of the nurses to say so. (This is the kind of politeness the French use on foreigners which translates as, 'not bad, mate, keep trying, you'll get there', just as 'if ever you're in Woking you must visit' translates in English as 'if you're ever in our neck of the woods, don't even think about it'.)

To be fair to these nurses I will own up to knowing some colloquialisms that are uniquely French in their humour; for instance, if someone remarks about the weather, 'il fait chaud' ('it's hot'), one can retort, 'c'est pas froid' ('it's not cold').

At a Stroke: Diary of a Recovery

There is a widely-held view in France that the English can't be bothered to learn French. (Only fifteen percent of English people can speak French while thirty-nine percent of French can speak English.)* English is the lingua franca of the modern world but it is not only laziness that deters all but a tiny minority of English people from speaking French (or any other language); it is also a deeply ingrained racism that is best expressed by the English phrase 'wogs begin at Calais'*.

'Wogs begin at Calais' is a phrase I heard on my first trip to France. I was a foot passenger on a ferry sailing from Dover to the port in question. Perhaps it is because World War Two had only ended thirty years ago, and Europe still bears the scars that cause it to loom so large in my mind. I am thinking of occupied France. The bright lights of the rail station make me think of the deportations, The Holocaust. The 'jokey' football hooligans' taunt, *Achtung! Achtung! Who won the fucking war, anyway?* provides a soundtrack.

From my French hospital bed I revel in the luxury of European citizenship and the rights it bestows. I take comfort in it. I think how lucky I am to have chosen France (or she me). I think about how much I love her.

Many people use the feminine pronoun to refer to a country but I love France as if she *were* a woman. I love her smells, her sounds. I love the way she looks. I love the way she makes me feel.

I love her.

*

I wake to the steel booted toe of a *flic* nudging me in the ribs.

A *flic*. A French cop. A *gendarme*.

I am in the Gare du Nord, the railway station whose floor has lately served as my bed.

I am with Andy Holt, my new friend from Nottingham. We formed a guitar duo within hours of meeting and have taken it on the road, busking in the Metro (the Paris underground public transportation system). We neck a coffee and plan our day.

On our first day in the Metro we learn to focus on stations with multiple connections. Chatelet becomes a favourite. (Forty years later names like Maubert–Mutualité, Les Halles, St Michel, Hotel de Ville and Denfert-Rocherau evoke the atmosphere and sharp odours of the Metro – stale piss, Gauloise cigarettes and a peculiar electrical smell.) On our second day we crack the busking thing. We earn enough to stay in an hotel (the Hotel de la Loire, rue du Sommerard in the 5th arrondissement) and to dine in restaurants. Looking back, these early years of my musical career were among the more successful.

Busking is exhausting work. You have to play and sing loud enough to make yourself heard above the trains (even though they run on rubber tyres). It is also extremely rewarding (in the sense of gratifying). It is terrifically satisfying to raise a smile on the face of a commuter who is hurrying from here to there, and who pauses to listen to you play. The sound of coins bouncing in a guitar case is a sweet one.

Our most popular song is 'Daydream' by the Lovin' Spoonful.

*

Writers far more distinguished than myself – including the magnificently opaque Algerian-born French philosopher Jacques Derrida – have noticed the entomological connection between *hospital* and *hospitality*.

> Derives from the Latin *hospes*, meaning 'host', 'guest', or 'stranger'. *Hospes* is formed from *hostis*, which means 'stranger' or 'enemy' (the latter being where terms like 'hostile' derive). By metonymy the Latin word 'Hospital' means a guest-chamber, guest's lodging, an inn. Hospes is thus the root for the English words host (where the p was dropped for convenience of pronunciation), hospitality, hospice, hostel and hotel.*

It all involves an overnight stay with entertainment in a place of safety. You could quibble about hospitals being places of entertainment but, as Ronnie Scott used to say, 'Quiet. We're not here to enjoy ourselves'.

While reflecting on my experiences of French hospitality (doctor's wife, mentioned earlier) others came to mind. I am hitchhiking very, very early one morning. A young woman in a small Renault work van stops and apologizes for only being able to take me about thirty kilometres up the road. She is the baker's wife and has been delivering bread. She takes me back to her house for breakfast then leaves me at the intersection of the main road clutching a loaf of bread. Her husband is very busy, but takes time to have coffee with me. To this day I don't think I've ever had a more delicious loaf of bread. On another occasion I am given a lift by a hippy girl with golden ringlets. She is wearing faded jeans and a spaghetti strap top and has unshaven armpits that smell of woman. At lunchtime she proposes a picnic. We share salami, bread and a bottle of wine. (I have always wondered whether the picnic had been planned for someone else: she was a sad-eyed girl who did not talk much). She shakes my hand when we part. What marks both these encounters (and there have been many more over the years) is two things: their spontaneity and that they were both initiated by women. I don't know if we are that comfortable with ourselves any more.

I think there was something uniquely feminine about these experiences. Writers on hospitality (male) talk about superior power as the prerequisite for the granting of hospitality. I suspect that, in a woman's word, hospitality is more freely given.

*

Yanis has more clients than usual today and is very busy. He nods to me to be seated.

I say 'hi' to Jeanne and take a seat next to her. There is a one-legged man who is busy pedalling an exercise machine. There is a chunky, sweaty man of perhaps thirty who shows off by limping around the gym holding his sticks at arm's length. He talks too much. He is one of those annoying disabled fuckers I would like to punch in the mouth. There is a very young girl, in her teens, wearing a gymnast's leotard. She is strong and lithe. I have her down as recovering from an accident. Yanis demonstrates gruelling exercises which she mirrors. (Yanis is an impressive teacher). There is a much older woman, very slender and with the skin of someone a third her age. Her hair is bobbed and I cannot take my eyes off her. She is neurologically damaged and her speech is very badly slurred. I cannot understand a word she says, but Yanis can.

She also suffers from impaired movement. Occasionally she will burst into exercise, bending over to touch her toes s dozen times, just to show she can, I think. (She likes being noticed). She is supple; her movements would be graceful if not for the motor impairment.

She has no teeth.

Yanis has me and Jeanne stand and hold onto the backs of our chairs while raising each leg thirty times. He has strapped the teen into a calf-strengthening rig and is doing reps with her. Then he lifts the chunky annoying fucker into a machine that forces him to walk (march, really). Tomas is there to help Yanis load him in. They switch it on and leave him for thirty minutes. The woman with bobbed hair is doing balance exercises.

It is an odd scene, cripples at their therapy. All of us trying to recover. To get better.

*

I always suspected that table tennis was gruelling.

But not this gruelling.

Especially this stroke recovery 'baby version' of it that is more like a game of pat-a-cake than an Olympic sport.

My opponent is Yanis. You can tell from his easy stance and confident air that he could be pro at this. I drop the ball onto the table to give it some bounce and strike it. Yanis returns it gently. I put my paddle out but the ball has already sailed past.

I chase after it. Bend down. Bobble it three times. Return to the table, out of breath. After the third time, I get what this is about. Yanis waits patiently while I chase after the missed shot. Chasing the ball is part of disabled ping pong. In fact, it is a key part.

*

If you have had a stroke, then table tennis is the game for you.

Name me another game that teaches balance, eye-hand coordination, distance-judging and lateral, forward and reverse movement. It also teaches you to be nimble and quick.

Plus it gets your heart pumping.

Once Yanis has succeeded in teaching me (via the try, and try again method) to maintain a rally, the game gets interesting. It is not as if I was ever going to beat Yanis; it is more that he is a reliable returner of the ball who helps me keep our little exercise machine going. (Lest anyone should be in doubt about the seriousness of it, on those rare occasions when we up the pace and I score a point, a competitive glint is never far from Yanis's eye.)

After The Accident my field of view is impaired. I don't notice until Dr Petitjean assesses me that I have lost some of my peripheral vision. A key thing to relearn, a major deficit to overcome, is the loss of eye-hand coordination. Ataxia. Or fucking ataxia as I unaffectionately call it. I am not prepared to spend the rest of my life trying (and failing) to hit a slow-moving ping pong ball.

So, I just keep trying. To succeed at it.

*

How many among us are blowgun sharpshooters?

Lack of accuracy with a blowgun is just a more sophisticated version of not being able to touch your own nose. It demonstrates an irritating failure of motor functionality; but blowgun accuracy is not a normal competency requirement. Failure at it is a feel good thing because this is a skill that no one can reasonably be expected to possess.

The difficulty with blowguns is not helped by the fact that huffing and puffing makes you dizzy. It makes your head spin. Add to that the unsteadiness of standing on a cushion so that you are constantly rocking back and forth between the balls of your feet and the tips of your toes. While performing this balancing act you are taking a deep breath and 'aiming' (however it is you do that with a blowgun).

Don't forget that you have first loaded the gun. This takes two hands, one to steady the long pipe, the other to grasp the dart and fit it correctly (make sure to keep the business end of the gun raised so your dart doesn't tumble out from its own weight so that you have to bend over and pick it up. Dizzy yet?). *Now* you're ready to try a shot.

Jeanne is my blowgun partner. You can say what you like about competition, that it is a good thing or a bad thing, but try and minus it from a situation in which a man and a woman stand side by side shooting blowguns.

*

Copies of pictures look more like original art when you make them after a stroke.

They are, to say the least, 'interpretative'.

For example: Eric places in front of me a worksheet with examples of the letter 'K' on it. There it is, in all its cursive 'K'-ness. Three strokes of the pen are necessary to construct this 'K'. I do my best to make it resemble the one on my worksheet. But it doesn't. I plod on, making more meaningless 'Ks' (I guess they would only make sense if you had the 'key' for cracking the their 'code' – if you had access to the original).

I do a little better with the lower case letters. They are less difficult to form.

They are simpler, less florid.

And then one day Eric has a change of heart (or changes his mind about his instructions to me): I'm no longer slavishly to trace the florid cursive. I may make marks on the page that correspond to the style of handwriting I actually use. Ah, progress. But maybe this is all planned, I think. Maybe the 'drawing' of cursive script was precisely that – a test of my ability to copy an image. Maybe it wasn't about forming the actual letters 'J', 'L', or 'P', but making drawings of them the same way I had to demonstrate as part of my recovery that I could draw a rectangle or triangle.

What else could account for Eric's change of heart?

*

Let's go to Khartoum *now!*

We're coming from Boston, so it's a long way.

I am crouched in front of a video game screen with underfoot pads that measure the pressure applied by my heels and the balls of my feet while attempting to balance myself. There are four of these games that Tomas has me play: skiing (it is giant slalom, I think), avoiding other pedestrians while walking, 'fishbowl' (what I call it) and Khartoum (what I call it).

Khartoum to Boston. Piece of piss. Using leg muscles I push myself up and lean left, shifting my weight westward. An arrow points towards Boston and I control the speed and direction of my journey by adjusting the pressure applied by my feet. I back off to slow myself down and hover over Boston. When I achieve stasis the machine acknowledges my arrival, then sends me off to my next destination: Bangkok!

With fishbowl there is a tropical fish emitting an air bubble. He moves about the screen and the goal is to 'catch' him in a circular highlighted area and 'hold' him there for a few seconds. I am crap at this game. I think is is mainly because I can't remember how to 'catch' the fish because I forget if it is to the left or right, backwards or forwards, that I must shift my weight. I really no longer know my arse from my elbow.

Skiing, sure.

Colliding with pedestrians? Can't get enough of it.

*

Eric goes into his office and returns carrying a laptop computer.

I am excited.

And frightened. This can only mean one thing: *typing!*

I have been printing block caps for a week now. Familiar territory where writing is concerned. (I am still making a crap job of it, but at least I am *au fait* with the goal, with how the letters are supposed to look.)

I think there has to be a fundamental difference between learning a new skill (which cursive really is for me) and remembering an already-acquired one (like printing block caps). Printing block caps has allowed me to hone a skill that I regard as important to writing, ie, legibility, making myself understood.

But Eric knows that I make myself understood using a keyboard, not a pen.

I position myself in front of the keyboard. This tool, the use of which has been second nature to me since I learned to drive: I wonder if I can do it.

The answer comes soon enough.

I fucking cannot do it.

*

This girl lacks physical attributes I usually find attractive.

She is tiny.

She is young. (As Randy Newman said in 'Lover's Prayer', 'Lord, don't send me no young girls tonight'.

Nevertheless, The Gymnast has caught my fancy.

I like the way she never looks at me except when I catch her doing it.

I like the way she rubs her palms on the front of her thighs.

The way she fiddles with her ponytail.

The way her breast rises and falls as she takes a deep breath before exerting herself.

I like the way she unsuccessfully seeks privacy by trying to pretend she is invisible while standing to one side resting between exercises.

The exotic flavour of exhibitionism which accompanies it.

*

You know that dream in which you are furiously pumping the brakes and the car won't stop 'cos they don't work?

Me neither.

Never had it.

But I imagine it would be like trying to type after a stroke: I do not have enough strength to depress the keys. I cannot press them hard enough to get them to work. When I do press them hard enough it comes out all wrong, because my hand has been hovering over the keyboard in an indecisive palsy and falls with random accuracy and weight distribution. The result is alphabet soup.

*

The problem with paralysis is that your hand won't move at all while the problem with palsy is that it moves too much.

How can that be?

Well, it's just like a lot of other contradictory shit in the universe: it is *contradictory*. And that is all.

It is about control. With paralysis you would like to exert control but are unable to. You would like to make your hand move, but you can't. You are suffering from a synaptic malfunction. The neurological circuit that used to connect brain to hand has been interrupted. With palsy it is the opposite: too much movement and uncontrolled movement. This is what separates us from the able-bodied.

*

You want to approach typing with something more sophisticated than a right jab.

This will require separating your fingers into independently functioning digits as opposed to a clumpy, club-like thing.

I complain to Eric that I only have two useful fingers for typing with my right hand: forefinger and middle finger.

'Don't forget your thumb,' he says.

Not really a finger, but yeah. As Eric patiently explains, my thumb operates the space bar.

My next typing avoidance ploy is to tell Eric that I will teach myself incorrect motor skills by only using two fingers to type; that my hands will learn wrong stuff that will be reinforced. He looks at me as if to say, 'no they won't, wanker.'

*

Eric signals that he's had enough of my bullshit, workshy excuses by shoving a text under my nose. 'Type,' he says, clicking a stopwatch.

I look down at the text and read:

> Le pilote d'un avion de tourisme qui survolait une region montagneuse s'est apercu qu'il etait proche de la panne de carburant.

Let's see: when this is at home, it goes something like this:

> The pilot of a passenger aircraft flying over a mountainous region found it was close to running out of fuel.

The thing is, we are in France and so we speak French. But I am still such a neophyte (at sixty-three years old) that this stuff continues to makes me nuts. No matter how hard I work at it (and I do work reasonably hard at in a desultory kind of way) I still find it problematical to think and speak in two languages.

Problematical doesn't really get it.

Half the time I am baffled.

Anyway, this pilot is seconds from *Mayday*. But I am many minutes from completing my task when Eric switches off the light and says *a demain* ('until tomorrow'). My typing speed was two words per minute (at my quickest, pre-Accident, I was sixty words per minute); but, as Lou Reed says in 'Sweet Jane', 'those were different days'.

*

Live long and prosper.

That's how Mr Spock would greet fellow Vulcans in the television series *Star Trek*. Spock had pointy ears and was a straight talker who obeyed the rules of logic.

I discovered that Spock's Vulcan greeting, which he described as a 'double-fingered version of Churchill's victory sign'*, is the ultimate test of recovery from the effects of stroke paralysis of the right hand. (Though I think that there may be a fair percentage of people who can't get their fingers to move like that to begin with.)

In hospital, the first test of manual strength and dexterity post-stroke is, can you touch each of your fingers to your thumb? When you first try it, you fail. You feel like you want to cry. It is gigantically frustrating to fail at this simple gesture that only a choir conductor is obliged to make but which we all think, *yeah I can do that*. We all think we can do it because it seems so easy. That's because it *is* so easy. All you've got to do is go like this…wait a minute…go like this…*like this*….oh crap!

The Vulcan salute is like touching fingers to thumb but with knobs on. If you can do the Vulcan salute, you have overcome part of your stroke-induced neurological deficit.

*

I wonder if there is anything more erotic that the hothouse atmosphere generated by French physiotherapists at work.

There are so many specific (and forbidden) elements that fuel the heat.

Cripple sex.

The intergenerational component.

The uniforms that are, at once, chaste and provocative.

Perhaps the most combustible element is the innocence of it. Everyone is focused on the task in hand: patients whose limbs are touched, handled, forcibly stretched. The white-uniformed men and women who are doing the touching, handling, forcing. It is this intense focus that introduces the possibility of other foci. The ability to focus (which applies to a sole object) is a precondition for the possibility of other foci. All are born of intense interest in the other, of intense passion. The passion that gives someone the power to treat cripples also gives them the power to check disgust. Checked disgust can be a powerful element of sexual desire.

*

What is the difference between having a literary imagination and having dirty thoughts?

Bless me, Father, for I have sinned I don't know.

Thomas Mann's novel *The Magic Mountain* takes place in a Swiss sanatorium. One of the most erotic novels of the twentieth century, its heady mixture of lassitude and torpor, of enervation, gives it an understated sexual charge.

Hans Castorp, a young man in his twenties who is suffering from tuberculosis, enjoys enforced, prolonged leisure (call it 'rest' if you want) in the sanatorium. He has, to put it mildly, frequent thoughts of sex (which are couched in allusive language that only someone already receptive to the theme would be alert to).

Fignac reminds me of *The Magic Mountain.* Our days are highly structured but lightly scheduled. We have a lot of time on our hands; free time in which our minds can wander in any direction they like. Relationships with existing lovers or spouses are on hold. You have already learned from being hospitalized that your main obligation is obedience to the commands of doctors, nurses and therapists. To have accepted this is to have grown increasingly amenable. You will do what you're told, when you're told. You've learned not to ask questions.

You are past willing.

You are eager to please.

*

So, they have a name for it.

Well, actually two names (for two different diseases): *dysmetria* and *hypometria.* This 'explains' (as much as anything is explained or understood by giving it a name) why, when I am shooting the blowgun, the darts over- or undershoot. Miss the target. You could say that

I'm just a bad shot, but *heh, heh, heh* I have the excuse that I am ill.

I suspect many people might be relieved to have a diagnosis. A confirmation that something is wrong, and a name for it. Call me old-fashioned, but I hate it.

I do not like knowing that I have a neurological disease. I don't like *having* it. 'They' say, better *the devil you* know. In this case, I do not want to, am not going to, make friends with this devil.

There is a weird understanding of the nature of invisibility that accompanies this. For instance, my paralysis is invisible, yet is evident from the absence of ability to move my hand. Even though there is nothing to see, the lack of movement (absence of movement) is itself evidence of the paralysis.

Dysmetria and *hypometria* are bastards because the disease is truly invisible – the result of a broken mind. A mind which can no longer function correctly. Paralysis is *sort of* invisible. The neurological diseases dysmetria and hypometria *are* invisible.

*

With paralysis there is no question about control. That is because there is no movement, nothing *to* control (well, okay, palsy).

With *dysmetria* and *hypometria* you have more than just inaccuracy, you have fucked judgment. No one in their right mind is going to let you drive the bus if you are dysmetric. (To be honest, I wouldn't let myself anywhere near a pushbike).

Jeanne is loading her blowgun. She has a bored air about her (a little like the Patsy character in *Ab Fab*). She rocks unsteadily on the cushion under her feet. She squints at the target and blows. Misses.

She doesn't react. Possibly because she doesn't care (but the more likely explanation, in my view, is that she is just being patient and figures everything will turn out alright in the end).

I load my gun and blow. I am trying to figure this thing (and my disease) out. The dart has landed well to the right and down, but is still in scoring range. I correct by compensating to the right but miss as my dart fails to penetrate the target and falls to the ground. I am a little out of breath. I load again, and my dart falls out of the gun. I bend over and pick it up. Now I am dizzy as well as out of breath and my accuracy is out the window.

Jeanne, on the other hand, has just put one close to the bullseye. Her lips curl in a little smile.

*

Brain disease is unspeakably creepy.

When I think of it I see grim-faced, tight-lipped men in white coats. I hear the clink of surgical tools. Nurses in old-fashioned hats hurrying past. I smell antiseptic. Thinking about brain disease totally creeps me out.

An orderly walks past and greets me pleasantly. I smile at him but am inwardly creeped out. It's like he's going to fetch the trolley to take me to my brain operation. (Just because no one's mentioned a brain operation doesn't mean I'm not having one).

To make the blowgun work you have to do five things: balance yourself, load it, take a deep breath, aim and blow. It is a lot of stuff to coordinate. It's a lot of stuff to remember, even when you haven't had a stroke.

I like watching Jeanne get better at the blowgun. It looks like she's smoking a giant cigarette.

She puts a dart in the big score area.

I got two in.

*

Pierre wheels himself into the dining room.

He looks around, surveying the situation re voluntary sexual segregation, eyes the thugs at the back of the room and parks next to me. We shake hands, introduce ourselves.

He is a handsome dude with all his limbs still attached. He is the other side of thirty, but fit.

His arrival has set the ladies all aflutter. There is a sudden drop in volume then a sharp increase as he leans over and asks me to pass the water. I cannot lift the jug with my right hand, but he waits patiently while I use my left.

People tend to dawdle over lunch in hospital. I don't (why would I?) and I am interested to see that Pierre leaves before I do. I have always felt that my fellow diners harbour unspoken resentment at my 'early' departures.

*

Surgery.

That is the reason why Pierre is in hospital.

He's had an operation from which he's recovering. Knee, I think. Right one.

He's in pain, if the grimace on his face is anything to go by.

I see him in physiotherapy. When he catches me looking at him he grins a little ruefully.

Pierre finishes his lunch even quicker than usual and is a little late for afternoon exercise.

Jeanne is, too.

*

I am early for Yanis's exercise class. The toothless woman with bobbed hair is hanging out next to one of the exercise bikes.

She is in pain. You can tell.

She pleads to me with her eyes.

I look away.

I know she is used to that.

She climbs on a bike and starts pedalling furiously.

After a while, she starts to whimper.

She gets off the bike. Begins to approach me. Thinks better of it.

Yanis's assistant Baptiste enters the gym. Baptiste is a spry, mischievous-looking fellow with a grin that is a little more superior than it is agreeable. The bob lady runs to him and points to her mouth. He smiles and puts her back on the exercise bike.

I don't feel good.

*

I am standing on one leg like The Karate Kid.

Well, a little wobblier than him.

Tomas is being responsible for making sure I don't lose my balance and come crashing down, causing myself a mischief. (I almost trust him).

'Close your eyes.'

I hate this. I instantly go from a little wobbly to critically off balance.

I understand precisely the reason for these exercises. I imagine getting in and out of the shower, having to lift one foot for drying. I imagine wanting to reach out and hold on to something. I know that there is nothing in my shower at home to hang on to. (I wonder if it might be wise to invest on one of those disabled grab bar thingys).

Tomas tells me not to worry and presses a reassuring hand against my lower back. I lose my balance and he catches me.

I fail at trying to stand on one leg. (Oh, I forgot to mention that Eric has me standing on an incline made of semi-squishy underfoot cushions).

I guess I have done more difficult things.

But I can't remember when.

*

Le pilote d'un avion de tourisme qui survolait une region montagneuse s'est apercu qu'il etait proche de la panne de carburant.

The distressed airplane. Again.

You would think that since I have now seen this text so many times it would become easy, because familiar. No. What I have forgotten, but Eric has not, is that my memory doesn't work. (I can remember vaguely that it is a story about a pilot running out of fuel, but the actual words escape me. Though I realize, as I type this, that the text cleverly contains detail that lends itself to interrogation and, therefore, successful remembering).

*

Nottingham. Wimereux.

East Midlands. Northwest of France (Cote d'Opale).

These are locations in which I have played Foozball. To these I can now add a third: Fignac.

Yanis has a couple of days off and Baptiste is looking after me in his absence.

'You know this game?' he asks, flicking its mechanism and making the football players spin.

I make a face. 'I don't like this game,' I tell him.

Baptiste leans casually against the table, continues to make the players spin. 'It's great,' he says. 'Very good for stroke recovery.'

'I still don't like it,' I emphasize.

We start to play. I ineptly try to mount a defence and Baptiste slams home a winner. (The sound of a Foozball goal is unmistakable).

And another.

And more.

5-0, 5-0, 5-0.

Baptiste gives me a look that accuses me of not trying.

*

Pierre asks if I will make a long arm for the water. I hand him my glass of apple juice.

Oops.

Ataxia.

I apologize, but there is no need. There's a lot of funny stuff goes on in a cripple hospital full of the neurologically challenged.

Mistakes and the like.

Pierre's request sends me hurtling back in time to when I would take breakfast in the rectory after Mass with Monsignor Archimbault.

I am eleven and a very devout Catholic. An altar boy who suspects he may have a calling to the priesthood.

Monsignor Archimbault is an elderly cleric who is the nearest thing to a holy man I have encountered. He is tall, a little myopic. He has an air of refinement about him that we are unused to in my small upstate New York town. He seems fragile. I have no way of knowing (because I have no models to compare him with), but I suspect he is also learned. Perhaps it is because he is not American. He is a French Canadian, a Quebecois. (The Americans call this dignified man 'Father Archie').

*

I am attracted by Monsignor Archimbault's priestly stuff: from his biretta (a square, three-peaked cap of Mediaeval origin with a red tuft on top and red silk lining) down to his purple *fil d'ecosse* cotton Monsignor socks (which, as a child, I mistake for silk).

Mass is a sartorial and ceremonial exhibition. I don my cassock (a long-sleeved, floor-length black garment with thirty-three buttons – one for each year of Christ's life on Earth) and surplice (a white, lacy, loose-fitting garment with three-quarter sleeves) and light the candles for Mass. I use the flame from a long, brass candle lighter (which is twinned with a bell snuffer). One by one, the tall candles illuminate the gloomy church. Wine, water, bells for alerting the faithful at different stages of the Mass are put into place.

In the sacristy I stand by the Monsignor as he dresses: cassock, surplice, alb, amice, chasuble, cincture, maniple, stole.

Showtime. I ring the bells that announce the arrival of the priest who will perform the daily ritual of substantiation, turning bread and wine into the body and blood of Christ.

When the sacred meal is complete Monsignor Archimbault leads the way to breakfast. It is always the same: apple juice and corn flakes, served by the Irish housekeeper.

*

Pierre gives me back my glass of apple juice and I pass him the water.

No harm done.

All is right with the world.

Again.

For now.

Until next time I make a mistake.

*

You're supposed to focus on infinity.

That's what they say about aiming a blowgun.

But 'they' (whoever they are) don't include employees of the reeducucation centre (who have no advice at all to give; I gleaned these instructions from *The Flying Circus of Physics* after I had already operated the blowgun):*

> With the blowgun at your mouth, look directly ahead, focusing on 'infinity' with each eye rather than on the target. Each eye will then produce a separate image of the target. Position the far end of the tube to be midway between those two images. The blowgun is then aimed in the correct left-right direction, and that may be enough for a nearby target. For a more distant target, you need to adjust the upward tilt of the tube, and that is where experience comes in handy.

The author of this advice adds, 'To aim a blowgun, experience certainly helps'. In the absence of experience, he/she writes, 'here is a further guide.' Sheesh.

So, the instruction is to point and shoot with both eyes open.

I think the French way of doing physiotherapy is brilliant. It is best summed up as 'do what comes naturally.' I don't think there is a 'wrong' way of doing these simple things.

I also think that the French 'method' is a good one: you are not encouraged to ask questions about technique which you will only forget seconds after asking them. It is like with French casualty staff: there is no useless, self-important chatter; no unnecessary talk.

*

Fridays is cripples' games day at the hospital.

The last class of the day involves a game that is new to me. A bean bag is thrown at ten pieces of wood (pins?) which have numbers indicating the score achieved in knocking just one of them over (knock over more and you only score one point one for each pin that falls).

The game starts with the pins arranged in a triangle that has one at the front and four at the widest point. At this stage of the game you only score one point per pin. At a later stage of the game (precisely when, I never remembered), the pins are spread out at different distances and the potential for larger scores comes into play.

If it sounds complicated, that's because it is. If the men and women in white coats were not there constantly to remind us of the rules and to tell us whose turn it was next, we wouldn't have a clue. (We don't really, anyway).

In hindsight it is remarkable how many useful skills are taught by this game: adding up; sequences (remembering when it is your turn); arithmetical calculation of how to achieve best score; weighing odds of achieving scores (by estimating distances, and force required to achieve distance); overcoming ataxia through repetition of judging distances; control (force and accuracy of shots); balance (you stand on yet another cushion); and, I'm sure, a bunch of useful stuff I am forgetting to mention.

*

Cripples laughing at one another gives a greater sense of freedom than skinny dipping (and reduces your chances of death by drowning).

There is nothing like a game of Whatever It's Called to make you piss yourself with laughter watching cripples fall about.

I think it's the fact that they do it with such abandon that makes it so funny. (The essential ingredient is that we in the cripple hospital are all crippled). Everything about being crippled that is likely to cause an able-bodied person to feel sympathy is celebrated with laughter.

I do not think it is possible for us to share this fun with our able-bodied friends. There is too much political correctness involved for me to poke you in your able-bodied ribs and expect you to join in guffawing at any of us.

The game of Whatever It's Called is enjoyed by members of an exclusive club. The price of admission is absence of the ability to make all your limbs operate properly. If that, in itself, does not provide enough humour, there is always the sight of those poor bastards missing a leg to give extra entertainment. (Have you noticed that there are no legless women among us?)

We are sixteen cripples seated in a semicircle. Yanis, Tina and Baptiste are looking after us. Yanis gives a 30-second introduction to the game for newcomers like me, then starts us off. Alain the one-legged man goes first. He wheels alongside the squishy thing (they don't make wheelchair blokes go on it) and makes a decent throw. Baptiste retrieves it. The woman with the bob is next. She gets a big cheer for her effort and beams at us. Tina has a go (in each game of Whatever It's Called a staff member plays, as if he/she were a patient). Being able-bodied (extra-fit, in fact) she gets no applause. When it comes to my turn Yanis pays close attention to my performance. I knock a couple down. Polite applause. Yanis says, 'Well done, Mr Trombley'.

Yanis calls our names when it is our turn (despite the fact that we go in sequence, most of us can't remember when it is our turn).

We go around a second time (this is the part where we can designate which pin we are aiming for and try for a higher score). I take aim for the 9 pin. Miss widely. My fellow cripples greet my performance with hoots of laughter.

*

The game of Whatever It's Called takes what is private – hidden – and puts it on display.

Highlights our disability. Puts it on shameless exhibition (*what's to be ashamed of, arsehole? Look away if you're offended.*)

Yeah, man. Cripples having fun.

Wheelchair blokes are spared the critical gaze that we turn on our ambulant friends. While full-blown guffawing is not allowed (unless someone falls over), ambulant cripples mostly get away with a snigger when they start to lose their balance.

And then you have the ataxics. There is a new bloke who suffers severely from ataxic cerebral palsy. I don't know how long it took Yanis and his colleagues not to be affected by the sight (and plight) of these poor fuckers. It is one thing for me not to be able to direct my hand to its target; it is another thing altogether to suffer always from random, undirected movement in more than one limb. I see it, but I cannot imagine it.

These people are severely – I mean *severely* – disabled.

There is a difference. Disabled is what we are. Severely fucking crippled is what they are. I guess that makes them *those* people. The ones whom Sartre (after Hegel, and in the spirit of Marx) called the 'Other'.

The ones who are really very different from us.

The ones who suffer way more than we (who are pretty fucking disabled) do.

*

Ah, fuck it: we laugh at them too.

Not to laugh would be to exclude them. To discriminate against them. For what? Being too crippled?

Give me a fucking break.

A game of Whatever It's Called offers a nowhere-else-to-be-seen tableau of the off balance: disabled persons on the verge of falling over. It is horrifying because of what it is. And it is beautiful for what it is: a demonstration of the healing skills of the people who work here.

We are the disabled on display.

But for ourselves. This is a public show in that it is mounted for other cripples to enjoy, but private in that only other cripples are watching.

'Only other cripples'. We are still people.

Public/private. We are learning not to care what other people think (look at those retards) or what other people say (look at those retards). A key lesson to learn here is about 'other people'. That's right, 'they' are the 'Others'. 'We' are us, and that is all.

The game of Whatever It's Called doesn't just teach us to laugh (in a tolerant way, never mocking) at cripples, it also teaches us how to be comfortable with ourselves. (I think some of us were not comfortable with ourselves before our accidents, so this is education more than it is reeducation.)

What is lovely is to see disabled folk with attitude. Cripples getting all competitive as they get better at stuff. Cripples who not only lack embarrassment, but who are cocky.

That's right motherfucker: cocky cripples.

*

I am entirely unprepared for my (ex-)partner's leaving.

I think of a backup plan. A woman whom I don't know well, but with whom I have been intimate, said to me that, if ever I called, she would come.

With the departure of my ex- I am totally on my own and helpless. (One of the first things the hospital authorities ask is if your home situation is secure, and that you have someone to look after you.)

I agonize about making this call. She lives in England. It is no small thing to ask her to drop everything at short notice; to change countries

(liking France for your hols is a whole other kettle of fish from living here.)

Kay Francis pitches up at the airport when she says she will.

*

The situation is, by any measurement, unusual. (What, you thought I didn't notice that you noticed?)

Kay is nothing short of remarkable.

She has a capable, take-charge manner.

She is jolly.

What is she doing here, volunteering?

(Why don't you fuck off and mind your own business.)

*

Every day Kay drives the twenty kilometres to visit me at the reeducation centre. (She is a consultant whose day job allows her, within reason, to set her own schedule).

She is now my *responsible*, my next of kin

*

They are thinking of releasing me from hospital.

I will still have to attend daily. But I will be able to go home at night (if all goes well).

Day release.

It means that responsibility for my care will shift from a team of full-time nurses to Kay.

Who would be her?

*

The promise of day release is dangled tantalizingly in front of me. It will be next week.

Wait: no it won't. It will be the one after that.

Finally, on a Friday afternoon, the powers that be (Dr Petitjean) decide that I can go home. (I was beginning to wonder if Dr Petitjean had forgotten me).

*

Leaving day.

I am packed and sat at the side of my bed. Waiting. The thing that I have mastered in hospital. The thing that hospital has trained me to do.

Kay arrives, cheerful. The nurses hand me over to her. We leave without ceremony.

I tell Kay I don't need assistance negotiating the steps as we leave the hospital. She wants to be useful, and is a little put out by my refusal to let her help. I have visions of the fall being worse as the two of us tumble down the steps, arms and legs tangled. Do I know that I appear dismissive and ungrateful for her help?

Kay keeps a careful eye as I wobble my way to the car.

This is not easy. By the time we reach the car I am exhausted.

*

Shall we go to the pub?

Of course we should go to the café

It is fully Spring. It is warm, and the air smells nice.

We have a glass of rosé.

And then another.

The doctor said I am permitted a 'couple of glasses' of wine per day. I interpret this as meaning three glasses, or half a bottle.

Tricky. But it can be done. It's a matter of life and death, right?

*

I do not enjoy being driven in my own car, but I know to be grateful.

We turn into the drive and my heart plummets when I see the state of the garden.

I have occasionally in my life been a gardener. But never of necessity (in this case it being necessary not only to keep the place tidy, but to keep it from being completely overgrown.

We agree that a man with the right equipment will need to be called. (I do call, and he comes within a week.)

*

We go inside.

The house is how I left it.

But with 'improvements'. Stuff is stored differently in the kitchen. It doesn't matter that I can't find anything because I can no longer cook. I cannot physically manage it. Strength and coordination are lacking. My ataxia is a safety warning. Looking at my kitchen – the site of (even if I say so myself) fairly regular culinary triumphs – I am filled with sorrow at the loss that it represents.

For me, cooking is more than a hobby. It is a means of self-expression akin to songwriting.

*

Kay is a very good cook (I am still a long way from being trusted with a knife).

She is a good (as the Americans say) 'homemaker'.

She is physically strong and handy in the garden.

She is no longer scared of large insects.

Kay's 'job description':

- Drive to hospital twice a day (and then, for an unspecified period once I am released and assigned to day care).
- Drive to shops and do shopping.
- Be responsible for keeping track of changes to prescriptions; sourcing and administering them.
- Make doctor's appointments (and transportation to and from three consultants plus GP).
- Ditto hospital appointments including tests and medical procedures.
- Organize and administer visits to blood lab.
- All associated medical administration.
- Tend garden (flower beds, weeding).
- Do laundry.
- Cook.
- Change bedding.
- Housekeeping/cleaning.
- Nursing.

Crikey.

*

I am too weak to do anything.

This includes mental as well as physical.

Two weeks after the mowing men have been, the grass is growing at a rate of knots. The benefit of having had it done (at some cost) is threatened with erasure.

Four weeks later it is out of control. I call another (cheaper) man.

Two weeks later I decree that I am well enough to cut my own grass. At the beginning of the summer it took twelve days. (It was rather like painting the Forth Bridge – as soon as I finished it was time to start again).

Now, as Autumn has settled in and there is perhaps one more cut left to do, I can do in in six days.

Grass cutting is my main measure of progress post-The Accident.

*

I am enjoying the gradualness of my return to pre-Accident life.

I have one hospital appointment in the morning (with Tomas, physiotherapy) and two in the afternoon (Eric, occupational therapy and Yanis, exercise). I take lunch with Kay (if she's elected to stay in Fignac for the day) or in the little kitchen on the first floor of the hospital set aside for day patients. (There is only ever one other patient there to keep me company. One is a woman who weeps nonstop throughout lunch. I wonder, uselessly, what private hell she – or perhaps a loved one – is enduring).

The days pass more quickly now.

My sense of time, of time passing, is returning. I realize that what I had mistaken for patience (in a self-congratulatory way) was simple unawareness. That – and the worry that goes with it – is coming to an end.

*

On a sunny Friday afternoon Yanis approaches me, clipboard in hand, and says there is someone here to see me.

He leads me to an office down the corridor and round the corner and introduces me to Marguerite. Yanis leaves and Marguerite stands. She shakes my hand and introduces herself.

She is a *neuropsychologue* – a neuropsychologist.

My first impression of Marguerite is not only that she is extremely attractive, but that she seems to radiate kindness. I says *seems to*, because – well, you never know. Why would a young and beautiful professional woman whom I don't know show me kindness? Competence I am used to.

She asks me to sit and begins to ask me questions. How am I sleeping?

Not that well.

Do I have pain?

No.

Am I anxious?

I don't think so.

She asks me generally about myself.

I tell her I am a writer and that my difficulties with it are the cause of great concern.

Ah. So I am anxious.

She inquires further and I tell her about my problems with language. I explain that the person who best understood this and seemed to possess the knowledge to help was a speech therapist at the big hospital, but it seems there isn't one available at Fignac.

Marguerite nods to indicate this is true.

So, is there anything to be done?

She will look into it.

Marguerite explains that she has a lot of questions for me and that the initial examination will take about an hour. She asks if that would be okay with me.

'Of course,' I tell her.

I cannot help noticing that she is gentle as well as kind. I wonder about it. I expected her to be competent. This is above and beyond.

When Marguerite has finished her initial assessment she shares her findings with me. I am not surprised to notice that she is correct. My perception – spatial and temporal – is wonky. I am aphasic and ataxic.

'I'm a fucking mess,' I tell her, in English.

She crinkles her brow to indicate that she doesn't understand.

'Je suis un futoir,' I translate.

She smiles and nods her head in agreement. But leaves me with the feeling that it won't always be like this.

We agree to meet next week.

*

When I return home from my *hôpital de jour* I am exhausted. I climb into bed and lie there, staring at the ceiling.

Resting.

I occasionally make brief forays into the kitchen for a snack. I look around the room, once my domain. Now it is ruled by Kay. When I open the door of the refrigerator she comes and stands guard next to it.

'What are you looking for?' she asks.

'I don't know,' I say. 'I'll let you know when I know.'

As often as not I will return empty-handed. (I just wanted to get up and wander – hospital corridors were better for wandering.) Sometimes Kay tempts me with sorbet. She persuades me to go back to bed to eat it (handing me a napkin so I can contain the mess that always results).

My fatigue is never-ending. Never mind that I go to sleep around 8 pm and often wake at two or three in the morning.

At first, Kay tries to keep my hours. She can't, of course. They are not normal. In the first weeks she wakes every time I do. After a week of virtually no sleep she is a nervous wreck. To say we snap at each other is to downplay anger, confusion, fatigue and the fact that we barely know one another. We soon abandon the courtesy one normally extends to strangers.

Then we catch ourselves and we pretend.

We give it our 'best shot'.

*

Kay is a strong worker.

She is tall. Has sturdy bones.

It is summer in 'the Charente'. It is hot. Kay has taken control of the garden. In the evening, as I fall asleep, I can hear her weeding, her trowel poking at the earth. I can hear her filling the watering cans at the tap next to the piggery. She walks up to the house with them, waters the sage, thyme, mint, rosemary, parsley, roses and the plants in the rock garden the names of which I either forgot or don't know. She makes three trips, a watering can in each hand.

*

I sit opposite Marguerite.

She asks me to mirror actions that she performs with her hands.

Easy, right?

She turns her hands this way and that.

So far, so good.

Until it isn't.

I can't recall (I am sitting here trying hard to recollect) which actions they were that I could not perform. There was nothing particularly complex about them. I just could not copy her.

My hands will not obey me.

Like all frustrated givers of orders I grow angry. (Not in front of Marguerite, though). I hide if from her.

I thank Marguerite for exposing my newly-discovered disability. (How many more remain to be discovered?)

*

I feel quite proud.

I tell myself that I have developed a brilliant form of physiotherapy through lawn care.

The first stage of development is my discovery that the push lawn mower can function as a kind of Zimmer frame (a 'walker' in Yankee parlance). You hold onto it for balance (walking backwards with it is not recommended).

So, safety first. As long as you are moving forward (not backwards – the chances of a stumble and fall are quite high) you are good.

Second stage is the fact that lawn mowing is good exercise. Easily modulated aerobics.

Cardio.

Strength conditioning.

Endurance.

And pleasure. The smell of cut grass. Measuring one's progress. The real sense of accomplishment that is afforded.

Plus the lawn needed cutting.

And, fatigue. There is pleasure in that, too.

*

Kay is partial to a gin and tonic.

Glass of red wine.

Crémant de Bourgogne.

*

I am being treated by Louise, the physiotherapist who occasionally stands in for Tomas.

She is called away to the telephone. When she returns she is distant (not her usual nearly-jovial self.)

'Dr Petitjean wants to see you.' Her tone is humourless.

I put my shoes back on and knock at the doctor's door. He is grumpy.

He has also lost his inclination to show off his fractured English. Which I find problematical because I cannot follow what he is telling me in French.

'You are a patient in this hospital and you are not a patient in this hospital,' he says.

As a student of philosophy (especially French philosophy) I am used to contradiction. But this has a dangerous whiff of the administrative about it.

'How do you mean?' I ask.

'There is no record of you being here. And yet, here you are.'

The little man is despicable. I want to formulate a clever reply about presence being nine-tenths of it's own proof, but cannot do it in French.

He goes on to say that I checked out of hospital.

'Yes, I went to the big hospital. Dr Faillon installed two stents.'

'You didn't return here to this hospital.'

'Yes I did. I'm here!'

And then I add, I did not come on the Friday after my stents. I did not feel well. My partner telephoned and spoke with the nurse.'

All verifiable stuff.

I ask for an English-speaking nurse to come and try and explain. But, Dr Petitjean understands well enough. He taken against me, and that is that.

I am dismissed from hospital.

Told to go home.

Thrown out.

In the middle of my treatment.

Particularly my treatment with the psychoneurologist, Marguerite.

Dr Petitjean dismisses me.

I extend my hand for him to shake. I know that he will not be able to resist the knee-jerk reaction of *politesse*. Too late, he thinks of withdrawing his hand.

I have totally disarmed the motherfucker.

*

I do not have my telephone with me.

I have four hours to wait until Kay returns. At 3 pm Marguerite (with whom I have an appointment) comes and finds me. I explain what has happened. She is shocked. Says she will talk to Dr Petitjean. (I have long been used to French hierarchy and entertain no hope that he will change his mind. She returns, unsuccessful (I cannot believe how decent she just was, going in to bat for me against all odds). I ask if I can continue my treatment with her outside of the hospital. Sadly, no she says. She shakes my hand. I watch her as she disappears inside.

She wrote down the name of a private neuropsychologist, but I lost it.

Footnotes

* https://www.quora.com/Why-are-the-French-sometimes-regarded-as-dirty-people. Séverine Godet is marketing consultant at ABILEO (Paris) / Editorial manager for Atout DSI. Other questions from this forum include: 'What is the most French thing about France? What is it like to be French? What do the French think of India, and its people? Is it true that people who don't speak fluent French will be met with a face of disgust by French people in France?' And 'Why are the French rude, or perceived as such?'

* A regional aperitif made from grape must and Cognac eau de vie.

* Graeme Paton, Three-quarters of adults 'cannot speak a foreign language', Daily Telegraph, 20 November 2013. http://www.telegraph.co.uk/education/educationnews/10460432/Three-quarters-of-adults-cannot-speak-a-foreign-language.html. European Commission, Europeans and Their Languages, June 2012. http://ec.europa.eu/commfrontoffice/publi https://en.wikipedia.org/wiki/Hospitality.copinion/archives/ebs/ebs_3 86_en.pdf.

* 'Wog' is a racial slur that refers to persons who are not white, ie, almost everyone on Earth.

* Wikipedia. https://en.wikipedia.org/wiki/Hospitality.

* Digby Diehl, "Girls All Want To Touch The Ears". The New York Times, 25 August 1968.

* http://www.flyingcircusofphysics.com/News/NewsDetail.aspx?NewsID=32

Dismissal

Dr Petitjean's dismissal of me has a profound effect.

I am a hospital patient. Stroke. It is what I am. And Dr Petitjean, at the stroke of a pen, has taken away my identity.

I am at the lowest ebb of my life.

That night I go home and drink too much. I feel guilty. It must be my fault. There must be a legitimate reason why I've been thrown out.

What could it be?

Perhaps one of the staff smelled drink on me? (I would take lunch in a restaurant or café).

I only ever had a couple of glasses of wine. That couldn't be it.

At a Stroke: Diary of a Recovery

Progress

It is 7 July 2017. I was admitted to hospital three months ago. I think it is time to review. Make an inventory of what is wrong with me (with notes on progress made so far).

Severe difficulty reading and writing, problems naming things and following instructions. For me, these are the worst things. But, when I think calmly about these problems I have to admit that I've suffered from some of them, with varying degrees of severity, for many years. For instance, anomia – 'word retrieval failure (ie, can't fucking remember). I can't recall a time when I did not have trouble with names. I used to be embarrassed by it, but gave that up several decades ago (just stopped giving a fuck). If I can't remember the word 'pasta', but I can think of 'noodle' and want to be specific I might say, 'those corkscrew-shaped ones that are not too fat' (fusilli), or 'those ones that are flat and very wide' (pappardelle). I suppose I am guilty of using a private language here, to which only subscribers (my friends) have access. I have a recurring nightmare in which I am brought to a hospital and and shown a picture of spaghetti. All I can say is 'noodle'. As they take me away I am shouting, *I used to be a famous documentary filmmaker....*

Three months into recovery and almost everything to do with language is much improved. The confusion with which my eyes greeted texts is largely over. I can read (but my attention span) continues to be diminished. Reading (think Russian novels) has always been about memory. Mine is improving from a base of zero. Perhaps my ability to endure a stroke was partially enabled by a sense that it was all happening in the present (no bad memories, so nothing to fear?)

Writing is difficult. I am fortunate, I think, in that what I am writing here lends itself to short, episodic bursts. I have not chosen a style; what I am doing is all I am able do. I can do it because each 'bit' is short. I can remember where I am. (For those interested in this stuff, today's word count is 344; it has taken about three hours).

A writer's output is measured by the number of words written (along with factors such as words per hour and so on – does anyone care about quality?) Having a disability changes the measurements (three words per minute rather than sixty-five). There are also qualitative factors to keep in mind (how long can you hold the idea in your head before having to admit failure and going back to retrieve it).

One of the ways to spot an aphasic is that he or she is unable to follow or understand or understand simple requests. (How this method helps to separate the wheat from the chaff nowadays is beyond me). I suppose this could account for me being fired from my mega-easy and well-paid job after my boss patiently explained and re-explained stuff to me in training sessions.

*

You know the doctors suspect you have had a stroke when they ask you to touch your nose. Easy, right?

Oops. Yeah. The doctor meant, 'try and touch your nose without poking your eye out.'

When you can't touch your nose without poking your eye out it's a sign of *ataxia.*

Ataxia is the condition of being, as the English phrase would have it, 'all at sixes and sevens.' Which is to say, confused, but, even more accurately, 'I don't know which way is up' or, more colourfully, 'I don't know my arse from my elbow'.

Ataxic persons cannot locate themselves in space. (We are the ones who suffer from phantom limbs.) The annoying thing about phantom limbs is not so much the residual sensation from a limb that has been amputated (how could I possibly know?) but rather the realization *that isn't mine!* when having a visual encounter with your unamputated limb. If you are ataxic sense that your limb does not belong to you.

One of the most common (and most dangerous, to self and others) signs of ataxia is inability to judge distance. The first thing we might think of here would be driving. But there is a lot of stress-inducing dysfunction to endure before we even get behind the wheel of a car. I will give some examples of common 'challenges' confronting the ataxic in everyday life.

Let's make a cup of coffee. We start by filling the (filter) machine with water. The first impediment to successful post-stroke brewing of coffee is lifting the pot of water so you can pour it into the machine. This is possibly the trickiest part because water is heavy and your stroky arm is weak. Much weaker than you think. It is likely to let you down just when you need it most. The trick here is to avoid mess. You are in danger of spilling the water (dropping the whole jug more likely). Phew. Got the water into the machine (be glad it's not hot).

Now we will measure out the correct amount of coffee. (I am right-handed). Grasp the measure in your right hand. Okay, this one-handed manoeuvre is well tricky. There is a lot of difficulty involved in keeping my semi-paralyzed, semi-palsied hand steady while measuring out the coffee. I can get it steady, poised over the machine, only to fail at the last minute. Coffee everywhere. Don't worry, you get three more tries. (Clean it up now, or wait until done? I wait 'til done for the simple reason that I am likely to forget what I am doing if I interrupt myself).

Having measured the correct amount of coffee into the machine is no small achievement and I sometimes reward myself with a small glass of breakfast Sauternes at this juncture.

The easy part: switch the machine on. Hmm. *Easy*, you say. This task is only 'easy' if you know the difference between up and down.

Okay. Time to get the mug. Walk over to cupboard, reach hand in. Which hand? My new, unnatural inclination is to use my left. Wrong. *Make yourself use your right hand.*

Okay.

With all this dithering about which hand to use I am now aware that I am slightly off balance.

Which hand to hold the mug in? Which hand to close the door with?

Coffee is ready. Decision time: left or right hand to lift the (very, very heavy) coffee pot and pour? I almost always elect to use my left (nondominant) hand. I am aware that I should be 'practising' with my right hand; but I pour the coffee with my left hand because it is safer to do so. Three months ago I wouldn't dream of pouring coffee with my left hand. Now it is my safest option.

I referred a few pages ago to the fact that I have become ambidextrous. I don't think that this is a good thing since it makes me avoid using my stroky arm. But it is a learned mechanism for self-protection.

For how long?

*

One of the most annoying (and potentially dangerous) effects of ataxia is the lack of coordination between left and right hands.

Ataxia brings fresh understanding to the phrase 'his left hand doesn't know what his right hand is doing.'

My hands are confused. They bump into each other. They get in each other's way. I go to a café. Order a drink. Reach clumsily with my nondominant hand and knock the drink over. The waiter comes over, I am apologetic. He says it was nothing, cleans up the mess. Two minutes later I reach for my drink and the same thing happens. The waiter thinks I am drunk or taking the piss. Neither applies.

Cleaning my spectacles is a bugger. I gather the materials I will need: cleaning spray, a cloth and, of course, my glasses. This is more difficult than it sounds because the materials are located in places like *up*, *down* and *under* (they are on shelves, different planes). Try as I might – and I have tried every day for more than a month – I cannot get this right. I make mistakes like spraying the cleaner onto the cloth, or putting my glasses against the spray bottle (as if by placing them there it will somehow cause the cleaner to leave the bottle and get onto my glasses). I am trying to hold three things in two hands and I am growing more frustrated by the minute.

When I first tried cleaning my glasses it didn't make me frustrated, it made me angry. I would say that, three months into recovery, anger is the thing I have to be most careful of. My ability to function increased greatly as I managed to get my temper under control. I think that being this ill in foreign helped immensely. When you try very hard and fail at something physical, it is innately funny – indeed, ridiculous – (you are forced to rely on facial expressions and gestures when language fails.) I suspect nurses judge us patients by our ability to let ourselves be seen as ridiculous, and that it is my foreignness which has enabled my progress, such as is.

*

With ataxia you experience disembodiment. I have already said that you experience the affected limb as belonging to someone else. I don't think I can put too much emphasis on how weird that is. *It's not mine, that hand!* The fact that you could even conceive of your hand as *that* hand, as not belonging to you, is alarming beyond belief. There is no nice way to be touched by that hand. That hand is alien.

It is an alien hand, it is creepy. It appears suddenly.

It scares the fuck out of me.

At best ataxia affords a view of a stranger's hand flapping in front of you while your good one is still attached to yourself. Maybe the one positive thing is that an ordinary wank can be elevated to the status of a hand job from a stranger.

*

A word of advice: if you are going to be ataxic it is advisable to bring several changes of clothing.

If you can't guide your finger to your nose, how on earth do you think you will be able to put food in your mouth without making a god-awful mess?

*

'Cognitive problems' rank right up there with paralysis as majorly scary shit. When you have cognitive problems, you can't think right.

'Can't think right'. This implies there is a 'right' and a 'wrong' way of thinking. Wait a minute, isn't that *judgmental*? Surely you mean *different* way of thinking?

No I don't.

I mean wrong.

Wrong thinking (I suspect) is more often than not due to a wonky perspective rather than organic disease. It almost always involves fear. We are frightened by things we imperfectly understand. Exaggeration comes into this. A certain amount of fear is healthy. It encourages caution. Too much of it is crippling. It will make you mentally ill.

Fear is almost always a result of stupidity, of attachment to false information. Anger is the bastard child of fear.

At night in hospital I would lie awake with fear. Fear of what? Of nothing, it turned out. I would grow frightened of things that, in the morning, were not at all frightening. (It wasn't as if there were no grounds for fear, there were; it is just that the fear was out of all proportion to the threat, which was largely imagined).

When you have a stroke you have brain damage. Brain damage is scary. There is no such thing as *good* brain damage. And you don't hear that much about *temporary* brain damage.

Brain damage.

Got to make the best of a bad job.

*

Getting around memory loss (in the sense of overcoming forgetfulness) is annoying but fixable.

There are personal mnemonics and, if all else fails, Google. What is beyond exasperating is forgetting *how* to do things. For instance, the day after my stroke I cannot use my computer to execute simple tasks because I can't remember the steps required (and the order in which they must be taken) to access the damn thing. All of the things needed for the successful completion of computer tasks require 100 percent accuracy. Even if I can remember which keys to press and in what order, my palsied hand will let me down with inaccurate typing. This is more than frustrating: it is infuriating. And the angrier I become, the less chance I have of succeeding. I lose control. My head is spinning. I feel that soon it will explode.

There is paralysis of the limb: no matter how hard you will it to move, it won't.

And then there is paralysis of the mind. There is no yardstick by which mental effort can be measured. Your brain doesn't sweat. Salt water is produced nonetheless – tears of frustration.

Today I am facing multiple challenges as I try to type these words you are reading. The first is getting my hand actually to move. It wouldn't at first, now it will (some). The more I work at typing, the easier it becomes physically to execute. But, physical execution aside, an equally challenging component remains: remembering where the keys are. Three months after The Accident my hands still pause in midair, hovering over the keyboard. But, less tentatively I think. Confession: my lips now move when I type.

Brain lag, delay, is a big thing. It sometimes goes on for so long that I forget what I am doing. Formulating the steps to a task is key for me. There is no jazz left in things. The white heat of improvisation is gone. Everything has to be premeditated if I am to have any hope of success.

I have to interview myself. I get myself to state my goal(s) (for today or any day) and then formulate a plan. Maybe I should have started doing this years ago. I am much better off because of it.

I often can't work out what order to do things in. It makes me ineffectual and unreliable.

But, you know what? I don't care. Not the tiniest bit.

Do you know why? Because it doesn't matter.

It really doesn't.

*

I am so attentive to my body now. I am superaware of what I think it is trying to tell me. But I am worried that in the past I have I misunderstand it.

I am the bloke who had four heart attacks and did not want to trouble the authorities with it. Multiple strokes, the same. Now I feel the slightest bit out of the ordinary and I reach for the phone.

It makes you wonder, what is it to feel 'normal'? To feel 'okay'? To feel 'well'? To feel right 'in oneself'? What does any of this mean if it cannot serve the purpose of being an early warning system for myself? Christ, suffer *four* heart attacks, each of them painful. What, do I not feel pain the way others do? Am I not paying attention? What is the *matter* with me?

*

I am getting better at judging time (in the sense of elapsed time, time passing). I'm getting more accurate in my assessment of 'it's three o'clock,' based on my estimate that an hour ago it was two o'clock.

I couldn't do that before. Nor could I make sense of the days of the week. Not just naming them, but understanding their relation one to another. If I keep this up, maybe I will be able to get a job.

Each day I make myself look at the calendar to check what day it is. I think this is the main reason why they have calendars in hospitals (the kind where you tear off a day after it has passed), so you can keep track of this stuff.

So, in the morning, at the start of the day, I can tell you, with confidence, what day it is. But I can't hold that thought for more than the length of time it took me to formulate it.

*

I find myself procrastinating.

More than usual.

I will think, 'oh, I must do such and such'. When I get around to it, two or three months have elapsed. Oops. Was it important stuff? Nah. Just pensions and taxes and shit.

*

I think that if you are really confused, properly confused, there is a sense in which you don't know that you are.

Confusion is a fairly simple matter. It is merely (I think in most cases we merely mean – I say 'merely' because there is another sense of being confused that is worse) bewilderment.

A difference between bewilderment and proper confusion is that with proper confusion you have some insight into your condition. You are aware that you are confused. To have this level of awareness you have to be hyperconscious. It is akin to drowning with your arms and legs bound. No. It is akin to watching yourself drown while bound. There is nothing to see, nothing apparently happening.

Just total cognitive failure.

On the other hand, maybe confusion is like shock. We go into shock so that we don't notice pain (physical, psychological). Maybe confusion protects us.

Prevents us from committing ourselves prematurely.

*

One of my favourite song lyrics is 'Good Morning Miss Brown' by Taj Mahal because it contains the line, 'If you ain't scared you ain't right'.

His suggestion that fear is our natural state has, within limits, something to be said for it. The lyric is set to a lazy, almost careless beat. It is like when I hold back the driving wheels of my push lawnmower and let let them spin – it feels like the spaces are filling themselves in. The song tugs with urgency, just like the mower does.

If you ain't scared, you ain't right. The song opens with a cheeky greeting ('Good morning Miss Brown, mama how do you do?'). Cheek accelerates as the narrator shares personal info with the purpose of soliciting sympathy ('I got the misery and the backache and my feets hurt me when I walk'). And then the appeal to feminine sympathy incited by small, furry animals and babies:

> The blues jumped up a rabbit
> Rabbit run for a quarter, quarter, quarter, quarter mile
> You know that poor little furry bunny
> Scared just like a baby child
> And if you ain't scared, man you ain't right!

It is hard not to extract a universal lesson from this song. But, as I say, *in moderation.* I have never met Taj Mahal, but I suspect that a man who can write so honestly about fear is probably not (very) frightened.

*

I mention 'Good Morning Miss Brown' because I think the song is, at bottom, a plea for caution.

When we get to the part where the rabbit shows those big ol' frightened eyes (we imagine them as big as saucers), we see them mesmerized, frozen in car headlights and we want to scream, *Wait! Stop! Poor little furry bunny! Don't cross the road!*

We are advising the rabbit to be cautious.

We are counselling *safety first* for the rabbit.

One of the biggest effects of a stroke is its tendency to leave a slow, cautious behavioural style in its wake. In your gait (it is more tentative now, as if each step is a question). In the way you stand (there is a tendency to wobble, you must be careful). Moving from place to place, you have to hold on to things (you must steady yourself). You have to look down more than is normal (you mustn't stumble and fall). When you get up from seated you will be extra aware of your thigh, calf and abdominal muscles (they will stretch, and they will be sore). Picking things up (caution). Putting them back down (caution). You are very aware of what things weigh.

A stroke changes everything.

*

I can see how a stroke might be viewed as a massive confidence-buster.

In fact, as I write these words, how could a person in his right mind view it as anything but? On the other hand, call me crazy: I like a challenge and this is a good one.

I guess the main thing is to have confidence in yourself. Can I do it? Can I face and overcome the physical challenges of having a stroke? The mental ones?

If I'm gonna do it, I must have a massive amount of self-confidence.

And I do. I am glad that I do. I know that without it I would struggle. I know that this self-confidence has its source in my atheism. In my unshakable certainty that supernatural stuff – stuff 'attributed to some force beyond scientific understanding or the laws of nature'* – is non-existent. I am glad that hospital is a house of science.

Having established that the bedrock of my confidence is a rejection of faith I can locate my strength.

*

Paralyzed with fear. The more I write this book, the more I catch myself in this cliche.

I know that if something is a cliche it is likely also to be a truism. But I also suspect that if something is so oft repeated as to be a cliché and a truism, it may be that it contains an element of truth.

Fear is the worst enemy (there I go again, cliché and truism). It is invisible. (I know some people say you can smell fear, but I suspect they are full of shit). When we are frightened, I think we have a tendency to grasp at straws (there I go – *again*). We certainly fall into sloppy ('careless and unsystematic')* thinking. It makes you wonder whether fear might be the source of paralysis.

Why would it not be? It is probably as powerful as love.

*

I love my stroke.

There it is. I said it.

Let me say it again. *I love my stroke.*

Why do I love *it*? (I'm not giving it a gender, you daft bastard). I love my stroke because it gives me a reason to be (even if that reason is to overcome it).

I am a new person now. I *am* my stroke. I am defined by my efforts to defy it. I am also defined by my acceptance of it, by my learning to live with it. (I do not have a motherfucking choice). Perhaps its impact on my life will change. Perhaps it will diminish. Or maybe it will increase. One thing is for sure: it is here to stay.

There are many ill people in the world and many of them take the position, 'I refuse to be defined by my illness'.

Okay.

I think most people who say 'I am more than my illness' really mean, 'I am more than my illness *before it manifested itself and changed who/the way I am now'*. Now, after my accident, I am someone who is paralyzed and confused. (I *used* to be a writer at the top of his game, etc, etc, go on and brag some more if it makes you feel better.)

Why not be both?

One at a time, or together?

*

Everyone knows that Americans 'overdo it'.

Doesn't matter what it is, they overdo 'it'.

I am in a French hospital. I am being treated by French physiotherapists. They don't seem very demanding. They don't even come every day. When they do come they seem to expect (and they get) a reasonable (at at least, that's how it seems to me) amount of effort. I make progress with which they seem happy. I guess because it all seems so easy – not effortless, but close to – that Americans might find it 'lazy' (not very demanding, or deficient in some way); as in, *French* (ie, foreign) stroke rehab. Stroke rehab *lite*. No pain, no gain, right? (*Hup two three four, hup two three four!*) It reminds me of noise as somehow being indicative of American medical effort, and I decide, *nah, not falling for that*.

*

Équilibre.

Balance. Stroke destroys it.

If you are like me you've already got a crap sense of balance before having a had a stroke.

(One of my main worries is falling off my feet). Stroke wrecks whatever sense of balance you had before. Face it: your prospects as a ballet dancer, whatever they were, are now next to zilch.

There are multiple causes of this (aren't there always?) including distorted vision, ataxia, lack of concentration, physical weakness (there are more, but these are the ones that apply to me.) For the first couple of weeks after my stroke I was confined to my bed, so I don't have much to say about the difficulty (or lack of it) while attempting to stand. When I did stand, I wobbled.

Standing on one leg, all that physiotherapy stuff, is, of course, difficult. Just standing on two feet is difficult. Wobbly. There's no better word for it. Of all the stroky things improved by physiotherapy, balance comes top of the list.

*

I cannot think of anything more tiring than having a stroke. It leaves you drained, exhausted, without energy.

It is an odd sort of fatigue. And not just because it is unearned (it makes you feel slightly guilty that no effort has been expended in pursuit of this fatigue). It is the sort of tiredness that is not cured by rest. No matter that you spend twenty-four hours a day in bed, it doesn't put a dent in it. I guess, however, that you would be even more tired (if that were possible) without the all-day bed rest.

Stroke is for me a restless sort of fatigue. Like the fire of hell that burns but doesn't consume, stroky repose is not refreshing. You lie rigid, eyes open or closed, it doesn't seem to matter. I tend to wiggle my toes a lot (maybe just to reassure myself that I still can). I have a choice of three sleeping positions: back, left side, right side. The placement of your intravenous drip (right or left arm – they change it every three days) is a comfort (or discomfort) factor. No matter which side your intravenous tubes are on, you and your hospital gown will get tangled up in them. (It is not interesting to then press the call button and see how long it takes for someone to respond in the middle of the night.)

A nice touch is that your paralyzed arm gets its own pillow to rest on (but space must be allowed for it when devising strategies for sleeping).

*

Three months after The Accident I continue to be tired.

I wake around five a.m., which is no change from my pre-stroke habits (early bird catches the worm has always been the 'secret' of my 'success'). After coffee I go straight to my desk and work until noon. I have started drinking an espresso around midday in the hope that it will revive me.

Trouble is, the fatigue that grips me is not so much the 'need to sleep' variety as the 'I think I'll just go for a little lie down' kind. Though sleep eludes me, I may not get up from this early afternoon nap.

Exercise: do I get any? Yes. Every morning. My garden is around two acres (one hectare) of lawn (okay let's not refer to it as 'lawn', let's call it 'mowing'). The mowing breaks down to about six areas, each of which receives part of a day's attention. It is a regular keep fit regime and it is purposeful, gets a job done that needs doing.

When I came home from hospital my neglected garden filled me with sadness. It also filled me with something close to anger to have to pay someone to cut the grass (which I had to do twice before I was strong enough to do it myself). I use a push mower (what is the opposite of a sledgehammer to crack a nut?) I am growing more and more effective at mowing. I am stronger. My balance is better. So is my endurance (when I started, I could only do about fifteen minutes a day, now I can manage an hour).

*

After my stroke I pay closer attention to what I put inside myself.

Last summer I embarked on a physical fitness mission. I started off with the intention of working out (in Nashville) for an hour twice a week. It soon turned into a daily (even twice daily) routine. I loved the buzz from physical exercise.

I am not a stranger to the pleasures of exercise though they are well-shrouded in the mists of time. I loved working out when I was a skinny kid in high school. I enjoyed my health- and vanity-driven workouts of last summer. And they were effective. I lost thirty pounds (two stone to my UK audience). I got my blood pressure down to normal and stopped taking the tablets. I felt like a million bucks, I went like a train.

When I moved to France it was the end of the gym and the beginning of my stroky time (oops, forgot to take the tablets). I am not blaming France.

My exercise here is in pursuit of getting a job done, so is economical. Eating and drinking are in pursuit of satisfying sophisticated hungers and thirsts. Everything in moderation, okay?

*

Weakness is a near relation of fatigue and the two tend to keep each other company. (Where one goes the other can't be far behind).

In French the word for weakness is *faiblesse* (literally, 'feebleness'). Here is one case in which the language with the smaller vocabulary is more precise. 'Feeble' seems to possess a diminutive quality (almost if the word itself is weak in the way that something shrivelled or withered might be. I also like the slightly accusatory, pejorative tone of it.)

Fatigue is a state you arrive at after exertion. Weakness is a state that precedes exertion and determines its degree. I am knackered because I am feeble. Simple as that.

Strength, weaknesses' opposite, is perhaps easier to define. Strength is the power one has easily (it's all relative though, isn't it?) to execute physical tasks as measured by weight or resistance. 'I can lift ten kilos,' is a nice, positive statement. 'I can't lift ten kilos,' is a crap and useless statement that begs the question, 'well, how much *can* you lift?'). Trying to measure strength by a deficit is disheartening.

Weakness can be lack of hope, giving up (in wrestling, *I give*, ie, I surrender). Perhaps wrestling is the best literal and metaphorical measure of weakness, the hopelessness that accompanies an encounter with superior strength. When I am overwhelmed by force – any type of force – I feel powerless. I might feel worthless (or possessing less worth). If I am not worth anything I am no longer valuable. I am not worth saving or protecting.

I think this is a symptom of depression.

*

Writing is a full-body activity.

You don't realize this until you suffer a stroke or some other disaster involving your whole body and mind. You have to imagine an activity that challenges the strength of your little finger.

Typing, when you do it right, involves both thumbs and all eight fingers. Catch a stroke and (if you are me) your right hand withers. It doesn't die, though you don't know that for sure, right away. You suffer some anxious moments while waiting to find out if you will ever be strong enough to type again.

Typing involves muscles you weren't aware of until you were denied their use. (I would not be surprised to learn that my toe muscles are implicated in typing.) Typing is exhausting.

Typing challenges you mentally and physically. The first time a speech therapist visited me in hospital she asked if I had started (she meant resumed) writing. I looked at her in astonishment.

'Of course not!' I replied.

In retrospect, my answer was easily understood (by me). I wasn't ready yet. (A few weeks later I would be).

How did I know I was ready to try writing again? I don't know. I suspect I had some instinct that warned against trying and failing before I was ready. How did I know? How does a child know when it is time to write?

He just does.

*

How difficult can it be to lift my little finger?

Feels like it weighs a ton. Or that some invisible force is holding it back.

I think it is the invisible nature of paralysis that makes it so unpleasant. So insidious. That there is nothing *apparently* wrong with you. (Are you slacking? Are you faking? Are you *having us on*?) The suspicion of dishonesty lurks.

One of the first things you realize when you wake up paralyzed is that the challenge you face is both physical (I can't move) and mental (dealing with the stress of not being able to move).

I did not waste a lot of time asking myself why I couldn't move, preferring to focus on the *what* (to understand what is, the facts; if we understand the facts maybe the why will sort itself out). Allowing myself to ask *why* might open the door to that most selfish and loathsome of emotions, self-pity; to that fatuous interrogation of the ultimately distracting fiction, *why me, Lord*?

I focus on the 'what' of paralysis because it is there that the possibility of progress lies. Identify the problem, then address it. *Why* is irrelevant. The answer to that question is either irrelevant because it is too technical and therefore of no practical use to the layman, or it is fictional (*God's will*, etc).

*

Speaking and writing are related – but not so closely as you might think.

Both use language, though in different forms. The difference between speech and writing is that speech is the 'language used when talking'*. Non-writers may wonder how much difference it can make.

It makes an enormous difference. It does to me because, when my right hand was completely paralyzed, I considered the possibility of dictation when 'writing'.

One difference between speaking and writing is that speech is public (which is not to say writing can't be). Speech has volume, you can hear it. Speech draws attention to itself. There is an element of performance about speech. Writing, on the other hand is silent. It is also private until you invite someone else to read it (or until you publish it). Speech is a physical activity; writing has an aspect of physicality about it, but is silent (its traces are mental). Speech is public; writing has the possibility of privacy.

I held off writing (ie, avoided dictation) while waiting to see if use of my hand would return. Actually, it wasn't just use of my hand I was waiting for; I was also waiting for the confusion to go away. Oddly, I could speak clearly (and grammatically) in spite of my stroke, but my execution of writing (typing and manually) was up the spout (words emerging back to front, etc). But I was determined. (I think it was as much my determination to avoid dictation as it was my desire to re-acquire writing ability that drove me.)

*

The act of speaking does not necessarily imply a listener. But it *suggests* a listener. With speech it is *possible* that someone is listening. With writing there is nothing to hear. It is not possible for anyone to listen to what is not said.

Which raises the question of intimacy. When we speak, intimacy is certainly possible (in what is said and how it is said). We can say of a piece of writing that 'it speaks to me'. But writing, I think, always has the greater potential for intimacy because it 'talks' to us inside our head. It is a voice only we can hear.

There is a kind of privacy to that (privacy is intimacy for one). It is also invisible.

Like paralysis.

*

Befuddled.

It means more than confused. More than bewildered, more than mixed up. It is more than perplexed. It means you are all over the place. Haven't got a clue.

That was me after The Accident.

I still feel this way a lot of the time, now.

Befuddled contains more than a hint of clumsiness.

A befuddled person will knock things over. I do.

A befuddled person will walk into things, collide with them.

There are some states that the French language is incapable of describing, and befuddlement is one of them. You cannot conceive of, imagine befuddlement in French. It does not exist. The nearest they have is *troublé – troubled –* which is not anywhere close.

I would make befuddlement a clinical category. But you can't have clinical categories for things that don't exist.

*

Get your ducks in a row.

Go on line, them up.

I don't know how.

Just put them in a row.

I don't know how.

Just put them in order, so we can see what we've got.

I'm sorry. I don't know what you're talking about.

*

Day One of Trying to Use My Computer.

Claire the nurse brings my computer. She flips the screen open and averts her eyes. (Her attempt to guard my privacy has a suggestion of non-physical intimacy, of shared mission). I can feel how heavy the machine is. Crikey! I don't remember it being this heavy. When she lets its weight settle and is certain I am situated, she leaves me to it.

Okay then! Let's get started.

An hour has gone by.

It's not just that I am having trouble operating my computer one-handed; I am having trouble operating it at all. I press the call button by my pillow. Claire lifts the machine off my chest. It is too heavy.

*

Day Two of Trying to Use My Computer.

I look at the screen. It wants my password. My password is…. Wait a minute, it's…. Fuck.

Okay, it's….

Damn.

*

Day Three of Trying to Use My Computer.

I made a mnemonic for just this eventuality. Sounds like *fille*. Sauternes. And there it is, as if by magic: Château *Filhot*. Okay. A vintage. Which one?

*

Day Four of Trying to Use My Computer.

What year? Not a vintage. A year. Maybe the year in which I bought my computer.

No.

Maybe the year in which I first registered it?

Yes!

Filhot2008.

*

Day Five of Trying to Use My Computer.

Need money. Bank password. I forget name of bank. It comes back to me in four hours. There is no mnemonic for bank PIN. I all I remember that it is numerically symmetrical, to guard against precisely this eventuality.

But can't remember my PIN. Only that it has a clever mnemonic. I remember I told my PIN to my brother in America. Maybe he still has it. America opens in seven hours (when my brother wakes up is when 'America' opens.)

Two weeks later I remember to call my brother.

*

Before The Accident I sometimes wondered what clinical befuddlement would be like to experience.

For instance, the language part. I would fantasize about how I thought aphasic language might appear (in the way that I have fantasized about being paralyzed from the neck down, like Curtis Mayfield). I imagined a child's alphabet blocks with words spelled backwards or jumbled.

It isn't like that.

Sometimes I can visualize a word. When that happens I will see (imagine) its correct spelling (in my 'mind's eye'). But when I try to type the word

I get it wrong. It is as if my hand is under the control of a malevolent force.

This is quite apart from mental typing errors which are accidents, the result of stray hand or finger pressure on the keyboard. Spastic movements. Non-intentional actions. But with the same result : gibberish.

*

It is fourteen weeks since The Accident and I still cannot type from muscle memory ('activities that become automatic and improve with practice, such as riding a bicycle, typing on a keyboard, typing in a PIN, playing a musical instrument, martial arts or even dancing.')* When I type with my right hand I mentally spell out the words and my lips move.

Clearly I am remembering these words. How to spell them. But I am remembering with my head, not with my body. I am not remembering with my hands. Not remembering with my fingers. It is all still in my mind, and requires a conscious effort to retrieve.

Words, for me, are not in muscle memory.

*

I wonder if people are giving me sideways looks because my hands are behaving oddly.

I have to think about my right hand before I use it. I need to give it advance warning. I cannot just reach down and scratch my ankle. I have to think about it first. I have to formulate a plan.

I have to keep in mind that my discomfort in my body is private (unless I call attention to it by making it public).

There is no guarantee that an ankle scratch is what I'll get.

(And if I am successful it will be as if given by someone else).

*

Where are my hands going in the air? They must be going somewhere.

Can they really be flapping about with no purpose, no aim?

I put my right hand inside my shorts. To scratch my balls.

Oops.

Missed. My hand is on the outside of my shorts.

No harm done, the itch is gone.

It's just that I didn't want it to go in that way. It was not what I intended.

I succeeded.

But I failed, too.

*

You panic when you reach for stuff and it's not there.

It is the opposite of comforting to reach for something and to have your expectation of what you think you're reaching for unmet. It is an unwanted surprise. It is unwelcome and unfamiliar.

It's not quite the same as reaching to pet your cat and pulling your arm back to reveal a bloody stump where your hand once was. But the shock value of that imagined surprise is not dissimilar.

Reassurance is no longer an option for you. Just because you reach out for something does not guarantee success in touching your target. Ataxia means nasty surprises. It means constant fear of the repetition of an experience, the unpleasantness of which lies partly in its surprising (unexpected) nature.

*

I think I have made a pretty good inventory of my physical disabilities.

Have worked hard at full disclosure.

What about my mental ones?

I'm a canny fucker. Reckon I can fool you as easily as I can fool myself.

But why would I? Why would I even try?

What have I got to hide?

*

I loathe Dr Petitjean for the consternation he has caused.

And then I set about devising my own recovery plan.

But I fail to take into account the extent and degree of my laziness.

Or is it lassitude?

I know I need to get better. I do have motivation.

Somewhere.

Writing is key. Continuing my quest to relearn how to type. Maybe do some block caps by hand. Maybe work at relearning how to sign my name.

Strength. Hand, in particular.

Coordination.

Vision.

I ask the lovely ladies at my village chemist if they can recommend a GP (general practitioner, physician). I fully expect them to say 'no' but they don't.

My new GP has dimples and a wise smile. She is clever and sensible of my needs. She is a no-nonsense, but pleasant person.

The nurses at Fignac warned me that there is a long waiting period to get an appointment with a consulting ophthalmologist (five months). I book it. Cross one off my list (two if you count finding GP).

My prescriptions (which had been written by my cardiologist Mme Faillon) are transferred from the hospital at Fignac to my new GP. The system works.

I practice typing. I follow my last lesson with Eric, making keystrokes with adjacent typewriter keys.

I set my own typing exercises: an Asimov novel (I forget which one) and Faulkner's *As I Lay Dying*. I in a couple of weeks I can hunt and peck with better accuracy. And then, one day, my hands remember how to type. Not quickly, but I can do it.

I am relieved. I didn't think I would type (and all that that means, vis-a-vis writing) again.

It is slow, laborious and intensely fatiguing.

You always hear about American patients rebuilding hand strength by squeezing a tennis ball. You don't see this in France. 'Fuck it,' I thought to myself and bought a tennis ball.

It was too stiff. Kay bought me an egg made of gel. It's yellow. I'm using it right now. After several months I no longer register 'cream puff' on the grip strength scale.

I know that I should be bouncing a tennis ball off a wall and catching it to improve my eye-hand coordination, but I don't. I know I should do tai chi to improve my strength and balance, but I don't.

I type.

It is my physiotherapy. Psychotherapy. Occupational therapy.

*

I spend much of the day in bed.

I am, more often than not, irritable.

After The Event I am, it if is possible, even more antisocial than before.

I do not want company.

I know that Kay does. But she doesn't speak much French.

What the fuck kind of life is this for a woman?

For anyone?

*

I feel odd.

I do not feel good 'in myself'.

What are my symptoms, Kay asks.

'I don't feel so good.'

She drives me to hospital. There is no waiting around. I am admitted quickly. They hook me up to diagnostic equipment. My blood pressure is high. I am there all afternoon while they poke, prod and stick me. When they are satisfied I am okay, they let me go. It is dusk.

*

Kay shaves me.

Because I am taking anticoagulants I am at risk of bleeding. (My hand and arm are are palsied and the lack of control is dangerous).

To death? Dunno. The doctors and nurses don't talk like that here.

But, I guess. Right?

Isn't that the worry? Death? From bleeding?

You don't know how frequently you bang yourself until you take anticoagulants and wake up one day with bruises everywhere. The bruises are evidence of bleeding under the skin. Fuck. There are a lot of them. And big ones, too.

They don't hurt. But what would I know about that? I had several heart attacks recently and barely noticed any warning pains.

*

When my brother and I were kids we would steer our bicycles directly into each other's path, courting a crash.

We would collide head-on, violently – knees, elbows, chins abrased.

Now, this childhood amusement would likely cost me my life. I might bleed to death because of the anticoagulants that are thinning my blood.

I look down at myself. It is hot. I am dressed in a t-shirt, shorts and work boots. Most of my skin is exposed. I am wobbly on account of stroke-induced equilibrium problems, so am (more than usually) at risk from falling over and cutting myself. If I took a tumble like the one I did two years ago in Nashville, in which I smashed my mouth, I would bleed to death.

Suddenly, I feel vulnerable. (I am not like that large number of Americans whose lives are governed by fear). But I do now think twice before taking any action involving hand tools (knives in particular – power tools are out of the question). Large bladed tools – shovels, for instance – are particularly threatening because their use can involve a loss of balance.

Everywhere in the garden there is thorned vegetation; the resulting injuries are minor, but the bleeding is persistent and makes them look far worse than they are. (But then, if the injuries *look* bad, because they are bleeding so much, then maybe they *are* bad).

And then there is the threat of accidents in general. What if I fall and injure myself and there is no one around? (Kay cannot surveil me all the time.) I could die.

I look up the telephone numbers of the various emergency services. Write them down.

Then lose them.

*

It is Monday, market day in Chalais.

Chalais is a plain town, not much to recommend it in the visuals department. Not that it's ugly – more like nondescript.

It has a good market, though. Lots of produce, lots of variety. There is a Vietnamese traiteur (egg rolls!) and a Moroccan merchant (harissa sauce, preserved lemons)! In my never-ending quest for good dive bars I hit pay dirt in the form of a joint with a Pelforth sign and a plain, Formica- and wicker-dominated interior from yesteryear. There is no feature about this place that would induce you to enter. The only reason would be that you fancied a drink.

*

I have always enjoyed a drink on market day.

When I lived in London I would go down to Smithfied meat market to take advantage of early drinking in the Bishop's Finger (in those days opening hour in pubs were fiercely regulated but relaxed for market workers). Same in Chalais (though France didn't suffer from Great War-era licensing restrictions).

I don't know what it is, but there is something exhilarating about going down the pub on market day. It has a whiff of license about it. It's as if normal restrictions are momentarily lifted. There is a sense of gaiety and freedom.

Kay offers to get the shopping while I stay in the café. I order *un demi*, a half of lager. And then the other half. Then I switch to rosé, nice and light. Couple of glasses. Then Kay returns. She has rosé, I switch to *pastis*. And again.

Then off we go. As we approach Bardenac, the village nearest us to the south, I suggest we stop in at Le Poirier Gaston. It is the only restaurant in the tiny commune. It has several rooms and a terrace. It serves a fixed price, no choice, six-course menu for €13.50 (never mind that the sauces and vegetables are tinned). It is also open all day for drinking. We order rosé. They can't be bothered with serving by the glass: it is €6 the 750ml 'carafe' (an unlabelled wine bottle with a plastic stopper).

*

By the time we get back home we are a little squiffy.

I am tired. I go to bed. Fiddle with Facebook.

And then I feel unwell.

I don't feel right. 'In myself'.

I can't describe it more, or better, than that.

My heart is pounding a little. But that, I think, is because I feel odd.

I am frightened.

I think it over for what seems like an age, then ask Kay to call an ambulance.

It is something I've never done before. I do not not take the decision lightly.

Soon there is an ambulance woman kneeling over me, shouting my name. I know what she is doing and give her the response she is looking for. She asks me if I have been drinking. I tell her that I've had a drink, but not that much. My symptoms are not drink-related – Lord knows I'm well acquainted enough with them to tell the difference between them and the intense weirdness I am feeling now. Something is wrong.

The ambulance team – a man and a woman – trundle me into the vehicle and off we go.

I am fascinated by the experience of being transported on my back while attached to an intravenous drip. The ambulance lady doesn't talk. I can tell that she disapproves, suspects my symptoms are drink-induced (ie, that I might be a time-waster and a drain on scarce emergency resources). So, I am not just a malingerer, but a thief. And an evil one.

But that is not it at all. I feel that something is very wrong with me. Something that has nothing whatsoever to do with being mildly pissed.

We arrive at hospital (our siren is sounding, but it seems distant, far away). Like it relates to someone else, not us.

Casualty. Again.

They begin the usual routine of questions while connecting me to the vital signs monitor. They draw blood, take an ECG. More questions.

Then they go away.

I know what they are doing: they are letting me 'sleep it off'. Instead of treating me.

A little girl is wheeled in. She is crying, quietly. She has a broken arm. Over the next few hours her drama plays out: X-rays, anaesthetician, nurse, surgeon. Her broken bone set. She wakes up, is comforted by her mother. They leave.

After several hours the doctor returns to say there is nothing wrong with me. He mentions that my blood alcohol level is quite high (he recites a meaningless number to me). He asks if I need 'help' with drinking.

One more blood test, another hour's wait, then I am released.

I am naked on the trolley (they transported me to hospital covered only in sheet. A kind nurse finds me a hospital gown. I put it on and stand outside, my ass exposed, while Kay fetches the car.

*

A local restaurant is having a *moules-frites* (steamed mussels and French fries) evening.

Kay is partial to *moules-frites* and gets us tickets.

It it is a landmark: I am going to stay up late (well, maybe until ten) for the first time since The Event.

It promises to be a lovely evening. We take our places in the al fresco dining area. It is a charming community event, in spite of the loud English seated behind us. No wonder they have a certain reputation as 'common as muck'. (Many of us are; it makes you wonder what possessed them to relocate to France.)

The couple seated next to us is an Englishwoman and a Frenchman. He, unusually for the region, is black. They are delightful and we converse easily, moving comfortably between languages.

I get up to buy a ticket for wine. Kay says she will get it, but I insist. The Event has left me very unsteady on my feet, and the uneven ground is not helping. The people next to us notice my disability. The woman smiles at me and makes room for me to get by.

There is live music and the band starts up. They are Spanish and make a very good job of Santana's 'Samba Pa Ti'.

I get the wine ticket and make my way unsteadily back to my seat. Kay smiles at me as if to say 'well done'. (These tiny achievements are enormously confidence-boosting).

The Brit behind me says, loud enough for me to hear, 'bloody English! Always pissed!'

The Anglo-French couple next to us frown. Kay starts to get up. I sense she is going to tear him off a strip. I stop her.

The servers bring our mussels. They are good.

We don't stay for dessert.

*

There is a fête in a nearby village.

It is a night one, and Kay says she would like to go.

I am in bed. Resting. As per.

I hear Kay slamming around the kitchen.

These signs of anger (frustration) are growing more common.

My heart sinks.

'I won't leave you alone. I'll get a replacement before I go,' she threatens.

She stomps out and speeds away.

Returns an hour later with a jar of honey. As if nothing has happened.

Who would be her?

*

I pull on my work boots.

Grab my gloves. Bottle of water. Sweatband for my head (stops it running in my eyes).

Go to the barn. Set down my gloves. And the water.

Open the door. Haul out the lawnmower. Fight off the wasps. Check the oil. Fill it with petrol. (I love the smell of barn, stale grass and petrol). Pick up my gloves. And the water.

I am very stroky today and my hands are not doing my bidding.

They are jerky. Tenuous. The opposite of smooth. Their actions are not fluid. They don't seem as it they belong to me, my hands They haven't since The Event. They don't even seem like the hands of a friend. They are at odds with me. They are fighting me.

I take off my gloves to drink water. I bend over to pick them up. Fail. Try again. Succeed. I pick up the water but drop my gloves again. I set the water down and try again. Succeed.

Now I begin to push the mower with my left hand. I drop my gloves (again). I pick them up and try pushing the mower again. I successfully reach the patch of lawn where I left off mowing yesterday. I put everything down and drink some water (it is bloody roasting). Both hands to hold the bottle. Bend back down to pick up the top and put in back on.

Give the mower three tugs to start it and off I go. I take my time. I am careful. I stop frequently for water. What a palaver it is, removing gloves, using both hands to drink, repeating it all in reverse. Everything takes much longer after Thc Event. All movements must be planned, carefully thought out before they are executed. And they must be done slowly, deliberately.

I survey the work I have done this morning. Not bad. It is time to go indoors, out of the sun.

The farmer who is ploughing his field not a hundred metres from me waves. I wave back.

I gather my stuff and go back to the barn.

*

I spend another two of my morning hours writing this book then return to mowing.

I am fascinated the boundaries of Martin's property. The layout is extremely irregular and it naturally divides into ten parcels with several microenvironments.

1) The rightmost part (don't ask me about north and south, I don't know which way is up) is a dogleg. It was the most overgrown part and the rear of it is adjacent to the unpaved road that connects me to the next farm, about a kilometre away, while the remainder of is it the farmer's field that is my back yard. (When I inherited these lawn duties, the grass had been reduced to only three feet in height.) There are a lot of blackberries out there.

2) Directly behind the house is my 'backyard'. A nice, open space that features a well-shaped walnut tree. Close to the house is a sprawling fig tree that is very productive and will benefit from a trim when I am stronger.

3) The third landscape feature is an extension of the farm field with all its unevenness. A barn opens onto it. Bumpy terrain, this reclaimed field. Eventually, I think, rain will help to flatten it.

4) The window of my study gives out on an undulating field that may one day qualify as a lawn.

5) The main bathroom window looks out over the area that features the *fosse*, or septic tank. It is not unattractive (and is verdant, as the ground covering a septic tank usually is). Someone thoughtfully planted mint alongside it, the lovely scent of which is released when the grass around it is mowed. Japanese anemones grow beneath the bathroom window and blossom well into autumn.

6) The house now stops wrapping itself around the property and we enter a new, cooler and shadier microenvironment. There is a hill that descends from the fully sun-exposed top of the field giving way to a permanently leaf-covered (well, mulch-covered 'cos I mow so often) area with a swing made from a truck tyre (a reminder that Martin's son and daughter were kids once – *tempis fugit*. I like imagining their laughter as I work in this area. I imagine my friend and his wife, Jean, as younger people).

7) We climb back up the hill until we come to the edge of the farmer's field as it falls away down to the road. There is a little orchard of fruit trees here: apples, peaches, cherries (all good for tarts, cobblers and pies).

8) The 'lawn' now falls away and opens up into a sort of meadow (yes, butterflies, some). It is the largest treeless expanse of garden. It descends to the road. The driveway is a border.

9) To the very right (from where I'm standing) it is more of a field again. There are apple trees and evergreens. We are at the border with the road. The post box is down here.

10) If we stand directly in front of the house we are at the piggery, a series of three ivy-covered concrete block and stone buildings.

I love this place.

*

The tank of butane gas that goes under the cooker and weighs too much for me to lift expires while Kay is cooking dinner.

She can't lift it either. I suggest she drive to our next-door neighbour at Batiland (a builders merchant) and get the lad there to help.

She does. He has helped her to the car with it, but cannot leave the shop.

She reverses the car close to the porch. She cannot lift the tank an inch. I belly up to it and give a mighty tug.

It is on the ground. Jerking and lifting, I manoeuvre it into the house. (I didn't realize that my resulting shortness of breath would last a fortnight).

Now, where is my vise-grip? (My memory is already shot. If you add to that the puzzle that results from someone moving a tool from the place where it belongs and relocating it, possibly to another building, then you have have some idea of the frustration and impatience that soon gives way to full-on, undiluted anger – not recommended to stroke patients for whom bed rest and a total absence of perturbation are strongly advised. Least of all because it only adds to the confusion that results from having a damaged brain).*

Having located my vice grip (it is in the barn nearest the house, not in the clear plastic tool box in the kitchen sideboard) I have to lift the empty tank from its mooring under the cooker and replace it with the unspeakably heavy and awkward-to-handle full one. It takes me a long time to figure out the front from the back. And an even longer time to attach the gas bottle to the tube and valve. In order to attach it I have to be able to distinguish clockwise from counter-clockwise. I can't tell left from right, up from down. It takes an age.

Three days later I am recovered enough from changing the gas bottle so that I can return to writing my book. But I have developed chest pains. I continue to be short of breath. My heart is thudding in my chest.

Should I go to the doctor?

Mme Faillon chided me for not seeking medical help despite having had four heart attacks. This was nothing if not heart-related.

I do not want to endure the accusing look of the last (or any other) ambulance lady again, so I ask Kay to me drive to my GP. She is away on holiday but her locum says, 'yes, get yourself to casualty ASAP'.

Kay and I are sent to Fignac. I am curious to experience casualty in this small provincial hospital.

There is no waiting. The nurse gets me admitted and on the gurney without delay.

I am giving an account of events to a nurse who listens very closely to me. (I wonder if there is a note of my 'drunkenness' in the medical record he is studying. Not for the first time I am glad for consolidated, electronic medical records so that I don't have to recite the whole of my history, including current prescriptions, from memory). When he asks me what medicine I am taking I hand him the *ordnance* from my GP and a bag containing all my tablets. My time-saving thoughtfulness brings a smile to his face. He asks me why I waited a week before coming in. Why didn't I come immediately my symptoms began? I shrug. I prefer being taken seriously to being suspected of time wasting (but, to be fair, I don't reek of drink this morning).

It occurs to me – it should have done before – that part of the medical staff's assumption about my condition last time I visited casualty was the olfactory evidence of *morning* drinking. How could they know that 8 am in Trombley time is the equivalent of their lunchtime (or ever later than that?) How could they know that when they are ready for a pre-dinner drink, I have already gone to bed?

I can see that my blood pressure was high upon being admitted but is lower now. A physician arrives to examine me. He studies my vitals and the results of the electrocardiogram they performed. Asks me to recite my symptoms again. He decides to order a heart scan.

I am impressed that they have such sophisticated equipment in a small, regional hospital. The technician loads me into it, the machine does it's noisy clicking, whirring and whining thing and then I slide off it and am wheeled back to await results.

I wait for a couple of hours. I revert to the passive, patient mode/mood that I perfected at the big hospital. I empty myself of all expectation.

The results show no abnormality. Good.

I must have one more blood test – it will take an hour to learn the results – but they expect I will be home for dinner. And I am.

I still have chest pains. They last for a couple of more days.

And then they are gone.

*

One day I wake up and announce that it is time I learned to drive again.

Kay says, 'no'.

Because we both understand what this means.

*

I engage the clutch, no problem, I am moving.

I drive the half mile down the unpaved road to the junction with the main road.

Three-point turn. Point the car the other way and go home.

Done. Piece of piss.

Just like riding a bike.

*

Next day I do the same again.

I think, *oh, this is boring*.

And then I think, driving and sex have this in common: they are activities that benefit from – indeed, are premised upon – repetition.

*

Day 3: do it again.

*

Day 4: day off.

*

Day 5: the main road.

I will drive to Bardenac. I take my time. Check, and double check, that no cars are coming. Off I go. Through the gears, into fourth. Slow down, this is my turn. Drive to Le Poirier Gaston. Turn around. Head back to Brossac.

There is a car approaching. I do not collide with it.

*

Something has changed.

It is fundamental and it has to do with fear.

I am frightened. Scared to death. There is no warning, the realization has come suddenly.

I am scared as sure as I am crippled.

Well, *you're not as crippled as you used to be* (got to look on the bright side). But I'm as scared as I've ever been.

Money.

Not so much 'money worries' as money terror. ('Money worries' trivializes a phenomenon that has sped past worry to meet with consequence).

Nothing has changed since my exhilaration at noticing I was forcibly side-lined from the business of survival except for the fact that I have run out of cash and credit.

No more money.

Never mind money in itself, who gives a fuck, right? But: internet switched off, lifeline to the world, cut. Since I was discharged from hospital I no longer have direct dealings with many people. The internet has shrunk the world so that everything in it is only a keystroke away. No money (the price of admission to the internet) puts the boundaries back where they were, restores all the obstacles.

*

Kay has suffered a breakdown.

Her father comes from England to collect her.

It is a long drive, he needs rest. He spends the night. (Top bloke).

When she is gone I will continue to hear her tend the garden in the cool of the evening. I hear the sound of her trowel in the earth, of her bucket as she waters the plants.

*

You would think that death – particularly a horrible, stroky one involving paralysis and helplessness – would be scarier than poverty.

But, no.

*

I am recovering from The Event.

I'm not sure I can recover from the survival of it – the poverty into which I have been plunged.

If only I could make something positive of the freedom from being able to 'make a living'.

*

For months I have been unable to work.

Physically (paralyzed).

Mentally (brain damaged).

But paralysis is largely over. It lingers, but I can do basic, unchallenging stuff with my right arm and hand.

I am confused a lot of the time. My brain doesn't work right. (It works well enough to trick me into displays of pseudo competence, but I know that I am mentally and emotionally disabled).

I am ataxic to the point where I am not in control of my hands.

So, I am as ready for work as a lot of people.

And willing.

Look! I'm writing this book!

*

Nothing makes me feel so alive as writing.

*

Writing is not like taking snapshots of events while they are happening (and so running the risk of not 'seeing' them). Even if your written account is given almost simultaneously it is always that ('almost simultaneous'). It is never *in* the moment. It is never *of* the moment. Writing, recounting, is reflective.

It is for this reason that the photographer is sometimes accused (unjustly or not) of not *looking*.

Of not *seeing* (because he is too busy taking the picture).

Writing (even if the account of events is given almost as they occur) is always the product of reflection.

*

The writer is the richest man on earth.

He is the creator of his own stories, his own music. His own history and philosophy.

*

This is a day that I have been simultaneously looking forward to and dreading – looking forward to because the vascular surgeon Dr Bastide is going to set the date for my carotid operation and dreading because I must drive, for the first time since The Event, in city traffic.

What I do not understand is that the correct object of my fear is not city traffic; it is highway traffic. City traffic is busy, but slow. Highway traffic is fast, noisy and frightening. It is all around me. I soon learn to stay in the 'slow' lane, even though truckers going the same speed as me flash their lights (I find this terrifyingly distracting). I cannot lose the picture of me dying a slow and painful death as the result of an accident. I am trapped by twisted metal. Emergency services almost reach me, but are beaten back by flames from the crash. My death is a slow one. When my mind returns from the macabre fantasy I am halfway up a Spanish trucker's ass. I realize just in time as the driver behind me leans on his horn and gestures frantically into my rear view mirror (with which he has nearly collided).

It is exceedingly painful, this driving, because every muscle in my body is tensed. I grip the steering wheel like it is one of my squeezy balls. This action doesn't ensure firm and steady piloting of my vehicle. Rather, it causes my hands to make frantic little steery motions and my arm muscles to spasm.

*

I exit the highway at the roundabout that takes you to the hospital where the nurses and doctors cared for me after The Event.

I am nostalgic for the refuge and safety it provided when that was what I needed.

I think about the skilful gentleness of the nurses.

I've gone all warm and fuzzy thinking about it. I have good memories of my stroke.

I have just nearly crashed my car. I don't realize that these daydreams (ie, thinking about my hospital experience or fantasizing about a car crash) go on for longer than I realize. I make a mental note that, from now on, for safety's sake, I should stop thinking when driving. (Judgment is largely excluded from this; I have found that my reflexes belong to muscle memory and have nothing to do with thinking).

I am nervous about finding my way to the clinic but I make my way through the narrow streets of the medieval old town without error.

The road to the clinic car park is very steep and very narrow. I remember that parking is limited and see a space into which I can fit. I take a deep breath and prepare myself to parallel park. I reverse in perfectly. Only I am two feet away from the curb (I have not judged this well at all). I attempt to correct my error and only make it worse. I am sweating and my hands are throttling the wheel. I eventually extract myself and the bloke behind me slides into the space I failed to take.

Next I climb an incredibly steep hill and arrive at its brow to find an open space directly in front of me. It is the last one. I was terrified of being stuck on the sharp incline without room to manoeuvre. My heart is thudding.

I walk down to reception and discover that I have left my documents in the car. I go back to fetch them. I put them on the roof and a gust of wind swirls them away. I recover them.

Then I drop my car keys.

Once everything is safe and secure in my pockets, I make my way back down to reception.

*

Dr Jean-Louis Bastide comes out of his surgery brandishing a screwdriver and explaining that his computer is on the fritz but he's nearly got it repaired.

Ten minutes later he is refreshing his memory of my carotid case.

'Left or right side?' he asks.

Christ. I don't know.

'Left,' he says. 'No, right. The right side.'

Okey dokey.

I proudly report that I have followed doctor's orders and have stopped taking Plavix (anticoagulant) several days ago. Expecting to be praised for my compliance, I am instead excoriated. I have misunderstood the surgeon's instructions. I have jumped the gun on stopping the drug (I have misunderstood his instructions). I am more than taken aback, I am overwhelmed at the vehemence of his reaction. He is apoplectic with rage and I become flustered. He goes on about me changing my medical treatment on a whim (as if), how dare I countermand, etc, etc. The upshot is that he refuses to treat me. I must first see Mme Faillon, the cardiologist. I know for a fact that Mme Faillon has no appointments available until next year because I had to turn down her offer of one because it conflicted with a holiday I had already paid for. Furious, the surgeon shows me the door.

*

What are the chances I will die, I wonder, while waiting for my carotid operation?

I only ask because Dr Gaillard, my neurologist, had mentioned that the surgery was not optional and needed to be done as soon as I was strong enough.

So, what the fuck?

I am angry with Dr Bastide for making me anxious. I am trembling. And now I must drive again.

Surprisingly, the drive home is less stressful than I imagined.

As soon as I get there I begin to write notes to myself containing instructions for the next day. First thing is to make an appointment with Mme Faillon. Her first availability is November, three months away (beats next spring). Then make an appointment to see my GP, Dr Janine Guyeau. Then write a letter of explanation to Dr Bastide (copied to Mme Faillon and Dr Guyeau, for the record). Composing these letters and checking and rechecking the facts takes hours. Exhausted, I fall into bed with no dinner.

*

I am worried about living alone.

I am worried for my safety.

The day after Kay's departure I write out a job description for a person to whom I will offer rent-free accommodation in gorgeous French countryside in return for looking after me and the house and garden. I don't get any takers.

I rethink. My main worry is safety. I have already resolved never to go anywhere – *anywhere*, even if only a few feet away – without my telephone within reach. Maybe I don't need someone to live in (the chances of them annoying the fuck out of me are very, very high). Maybe I just need a char, half a day fortnightly.

I am pretty sure that the lady who owns our local shop can help. Indeed, she can. She gives me the name of a woman who sounds very nice on the phone but can only accept one full day of employment, weekly.

I decide to knuckle down and do my own housework.

Footnotes

* *OED.*

* *OED.*

* *Collins English Dictionary.*

* *Wikipedia.*

* Nor did I realize that searching for misplaced items would now become a grossly irritating feature of daily life. I calm myself by reflecting that, for every misplaced object there is bound to be a compensating reward in some other department.

Recovery

It's not that I dislike housework.

There are times when I positively enjoy it.

But I don't know if I am capable of doing it now. Am I strong enough? Do I possess the ability to maintain my balance and not fall and injure myself? Do I have enough stamina to complete tasks?

I will find out by trying.

I start with the bedroom, where I spend most of my time.

Day one. Clear stuff out of the way and vacuum. This part takes nearly two hours. I stop frequently to rest. I move rugs and vacuum under them. I start to run the vacuum brush into the corners and soon discover that spiders and big, big cobwebs, are lurking. In fact, they are everywhere, funny how I hadn't noticed them while lying in bed.

Corners lead to walls which lead to ceilings which lead to more walls and more ceilings. And more cobwebs.

Time for lunch. I cannot relax to eat it. I wolf it down as if I've a gun to my head. This is all a part of hurrying through a task which normally would take a couple of hours but, post-The Event, is going to take all day.

Eventually I get to the penultimate part of the job: mopping. It is wonderfully satisfying.

I have cleared everything to one side of the room in preparation. I love the splash of the mop plunging into the water, the sound of it dripping as I twist the excess water out of it, and the satisfying way the head glides over the grimy surface, restoring the paintwork to a state of cleanliness. I rest while it dries. I move the rugs and do the other half. Rest, let it dry. Reassemble the room.

It is immensely satisfying. Okay, the sun has gone down, it's taken all day. But *I* did it. Not a helper, not the cleaning lady, *me*.

I did it.

*

I am on a cleaning jag and you couldn't stop me if you wanted to.

Today I am going to launder the sheets and pillowcases. It's been two weeks – long enough. (It would be nice to do it every week, but I don't think I am up to it).

Yesterday's effort tired me. It's not like exercising with weights, for example, which makes you tired but builds strength. Housework just makes you tired and that is it. There are no benefits (apart from having a clean house) at the end of it.

The laundry is a challenge (it's a bugger, actually) since I've started taking blood thinners. I bleed all the time, everywhere, with the slightest provocation. I bleed at night when I don't know that I'm doing it. Kay was really good at getting the blood out of sheets. I am crap at it.

Stripping the bed and washing the sheets is no big deal. Putting the bedding back together is. I have always dreaded putting the duvet back on. Fitted sheets are okay, and even the pillowcases, which are a tight fit, aren't too bad. But I have always found duvets awkward and now that I am ataxic they are impossible. It is like trying to explain to someone who has no sense of up, down or inside-out (me) what is up, down and inside-out. The frustration it induces is nearly unbearable.

And it takes forever.

I loathe it.

*

Once I start with the housework, I cannot stop.

It is like with the lawn mowing, I can't stop. I must not allow it to become an obsession.

Don't worry – it hasn't. Last week I let the dishes pile up for three days; man, it felt good to let stuff go!

I make a list of cleaning chores that must be done, and a schedule devoting one day a week to them. But I am impatient to get on with it, so I assign myself chores every other day. I vacuum and scrub the bathrooms until their enamel shines like new. I take the spare room apart and clean every inch of it. I spend two days on the kitchen. I do a thorough clean of my study, the living room, the laundry room.

Now they are all clean I can do the necessary to maintain them (knowing full well that I will revert to my pre-Event ways and ignore these tasks until the filth becomes unbearable).

I think I am getting better.

*

So, how are you, Stephen?

Never better, what about you?

Whaddya mean, 'never better?'

What I said.

How can you be 'never better' when you clearly have been better.

Ah, but that was then and this is now. I could say 'I used to be fitter thirty years ago but I won't 'cos it isn't what you asked me.'

But don't you regret losing full use of your limbs?

What is that? You are taking about stuff that happened before the event. There is no 'before the event' anymore. It doesn't exist. There is just me, my stroky self.

So I guess you're grateful for what mobility you've got left?

Grateful? To whom? To what? No one, no thing *gave* me my mobility. I *have* mobility or I *don't have* mobility. I *possess* it or I *don't possess* it. It is *mine*. I lost much of it for a bit. Now I am missing part of it. I cannot pretend to feelings of gratitude for what cannot be given or taken away.

Well…

Chill, dude. I'm *never better.*